WORLD WAR I
MINNESOTA

WORLD WAR I
MINNESOTA

.... ★ ....

Iric Nathanson

THE
History
PRESS

Published by The History Press
Charleston, SC
www.historypress.net

Copyright © 2016 by Iric Nathanson
All rights reserved

First published 2016

Manufactured in the United States

ISBN 978.1.46711.792.0

Library of Congress Control Number: 2015953415

For Marlene

CONTENTS

ACKNOWLEDGEMENTS

O ver these past two years, I was able to draw on the help of many people as this book moved from the idea stage to the finished product. Staffs from archival agencies throughout Minnesota helped locate the images that made the story of World War I in Minnesota more vivid. They included Ted Hathaway and his team at the Hennepin County Library Special Collections, Susan Hoffman at the University of Minnesota Archives, Darla Gebhard from the Brown County Historical Society, Patricia Maus and Mags David from the Katherine A. Martin Archives at the University of Minnesota Duluth and Ellen Holt-Werle at the Macalester College Archives.

My friend Bill Skelton shared his expertise, gained over a long career as a professor of American history at the University of Wisconsin Stevens Point. My neighbor Carol Masters and my wife, Marlene, used their red pencils—but did so gently—to copy-edit my text.

And finally, acquisitions editor Greg Dumais at The History Press fielded my numerous early morning phone calls and kept me on track as this book came together.

My heartfelt thanks to all of you.

INTRODUCTION

"E rst schaff dein Sach, Dann trink and lach." In English, it means "First do your duty, then drink and laugh."

This cheerful German proverb and more than twenty others like it, ornamented in old Germanic script, decorate the walls of a unique space in the basement of Minnesota's state capitol, the rathskeller, a small café open to the public when the Minnesota legislature is in session.[1]

The German sayings first appeared in the capitol in 1905 to honor Minnesota's German Americans, then the state's largest ethnic group. But twelve years later, on orders from Governor J.A.A. Burnquist, the innocent proverbs were painted over with layers of white paint to obscure their Germanic identity. The year was 1917. The United States had just entered World War I. With the temperance movement gaining momentum at home, German language signs promoting alcohol consumption had become offensive.

This country had entered the Great War, as it was known then, after the massive military struggle had been underway for three years. In 1914, when the first shots were fired on the European battlefields, the war seemed remote and of little relevance for many Minnesotans.

In the eastern United States, reports of so-called German atrocities generated widespread support for the Triple Entente powers of Britain, France and Russia. However, in the Midwest, according to historians Franklin Holbrook and Livia Appel, "disapproval of Germany continued to be tempered for a long time by the prevailing sense of remoteness from the stage of conflict, lack of concern over the issues at stake, the pacific sentiments of the Scandinavian element and the openly expressed sympathy of the large body of German Americans."[2]

With the U.S. declaration of war in April 1917, public opinion took a sharp turn in Minnesota. The Germans—the Huns as they were now called—had become this country's sworn enemies. In his order calling for the obliteration of the capitol's harmless German slogans, Burnquist's action was symptomatic of the nativist sentiment sweeping through a state just coming to terms with a war that would draw thousands of young Minnesotans to the European battlefields. Two decades later, even more young Minnesotans, many the sons of World War I veterans, would find themselves on the front lines of another worldwide military conflict.

On the surface, there were many similarities between life on the homefront during the two wartime eras. In World War I and again in World War II, Minnesotans demonstrated their patriotism and their support for the boys who were doing the fighting "over there." Friends and neighbors back home were able to back the war effort by buying war bonds, volunteering with the Red Cross and conserving food and other scarce resources.

Despite these similarities, there were significant differences in Minnesota's political and social mood during the two wartime eras, separated by only twenty-two years. In 1939, the shock of Pearl Harbor unified the country and ended any real dissent about this country's need to go to war in support of its European allies. Two decades earlier, the run-up to war had been a lot less sudden. True, Americans had been victims of German submarine attacks in the North Atlantic as far back as 1915, when the British ocean liner the *Lusitania* was sunk by German torpedoes. But the U.S. declaration of war in the spring of 1917 came at a time when a substantial segment of American public opinion was still in favor of neutrality—nationally and here in Minnesota. This view was reflected in the votes of three Minnesota congressmen who opposed President Wilson's war resolution when the measure came before the U.S. House on April 6.

All three lawmakers represented congressional districts with sizable numbers of German Americans, many of whom were first generation immigrants with close ties to their homeland. While the overwhelming majority of these new Minnesotans professed their loyalty to the United States and their support for the war effort, some state opinion makers, who considered themselves "100 percent Americans," were convinced that German Americans were harboring a massive fifth column in Minnesota.

These suspicions helped create a dark undertone to the calls for state residents to demonstrate their patriotism. This undertone was reinforced by a powerful but short-lived state agency known as the Commission of Public Safety. The commission was organized in 1917 to mobilize support for the war and clamp down on dissent. In its disregard for civil liberties, the Minnesota commission represented a state precursor to the U.S. House Committee on Un-American Activities, established twenty years later, in 1938.

While anti-German sentiment in Minnesota during World War I never reached the level of enmity expressed toward Japanese Americans on the West Coast in the 1940s, it came close. In the largely German American community of New Ulm in southern Minnesota, two local officials were removed from office by the Public Safety Commission on grounds that their reservations about the military draft constituted disloyalty.

While the commission was contending with what it viewed as unpatriotic opinions expressed by some German Americans, it was facing other threats to the existing political and social order in Minnesota. The advent of war in 1917 coincided with the emergence of a major new political force that was sweeping into Minnesota from the west. Identified by the deceptively benign label as the Nonpartisan League, this left-leaning political movement had captured control of North Dakota's government in 1916.

The league's program called for the establishment of a state-owned bank, strict regulation of railroad rates and other populist measures designed to appeal to local farmers, who constituted the state's largest population group. North Dakota's independent-minded farmers had long chafed under what they viewed as the heavy-handed treatment by the railroads, banks and grain merchants headquartered in Minnesota's two major cites of Minneapolis and St. Paul.

Now, at a time when the nation was at war, the league was rapidly gaining support in Minnesota's rural districts. This political development posed a serious threat to the very economic interests centered in the Twin Cities that had been the movement's targets in North Dakota.

The league's leaders, including former Minnesota congressman Charles Lindbergh, generally voiced their support for the war but called attention to the big-business interests who sought to benefit from it. In 1918, Lindbergh, the father of the famous aviator, received league backing for his efforts to unseat Burnquist, the state's incumbent governor, in the June Republican primary.

Minnesota's corporate interests viewed the Nonpartisan League and its left-leaning platform with alarm. For them, a Lindbergh victory raised the specter of a socialist takeover of state government. The U.S. entrance into World War I gave these interests a convenient weapon they could use in their battle with Lindbergh and his league supporters. Ignoring Lindbergh's claims that he did, in fact, support this country's military efforts in Europe, Burnquist's backers focused on Lindbergh's prewar statements, which questioned the motivations for U.S. involvement in the European military conflict.

The substantive issues separating the candidates in 1918 might have been local in nature, but Lindbergh's opponents used the war to drive a wedge between his left-leaning supporters and those segments of his political base that might have agreed with the former congressman's economic program but were reluctant to support him for fear of being seen as disloyal and unpatriotic.

In Minneapolis, the city's socialist mayor, Thomas Van Lear, shared Lindbergh's views about the war and the economic interests that were encouraging it. And, like Lindberg, Van Lear found that his opponents were using the loyalty issue to weaken the mayor's strong support in the city's working-class neighborhoods. While Van Lear, elected in 1916, would voice his support for the U.S. military effort after war was declared in 1917, his Socialist Party of America at the national level remained firmly opposed to the war. To the left of the socialists, the militant Industrial Workers of the World (IWW) had established a foothold in the mining district of northern Minnesota. There, some Wobblies, as they were known, made veiled threats to sabotage the war effort. These threats provided effective campaign fodder for those conservative interests who were determined to halt Minnesota's leftward drift.

The issue of wartime preparedness spilled over into the economic sphere during a bitter strike by workers at the Twin City Rapid Transit Company in 1917. Here again, the Public Safety Commission intervened on grounds that the strike impeded the war effort by disrupting the transportation system that brought workers to the jobs in the local defense plants.

As these political, social and economic forces buffeted the state, the need for homefront mobilization was, at times, expressed in coercive tones that seem threatening to those who harbored some reservations about the war. In certain communities, German Americans were challenged to demonstrate their 100 percent Americanism by purchasing war bonds. In other places, failure to display the American flag was viewed as unpatriotic. In the Twin Cities, workers were told that support for militant unionism was a "slap in the face" at the boys who were "over there" fighting for their country in the battlefield trenches.

While the Minnesota homefront might have been roiled by impact of the war, the agitation was short-lived. In the fall of 1918, the war was winding down, just as this state and the rest of the world were caught up in the worldwide influenza pandemic, a deadly scourge that would claim ten times as many American lives as those taken on the European battlefields. Then, on November 11, only a year and half after the United States entered the war, an armistice was signed and the conflict was over. In Minnesota, homefront mobilization came to a halt, the Public Safety Commission was disbanded and life returned to a more placid prewar pace as the decade of the 1920s approached.

On the political front, the elections of 1918 halted Minnesota's move to the left—at least temporarily. But over the longer term, that year's pivotal election laid the groundwork for a labor-agrarian alliance that would propel a major new political movement in Minnesota.

In the immediate postwar years, this state and the rest of country were caught up in the so-called red scare, which targeted individuals and political groups accused of harboring pro-Communist sentiments.

The election of 1920 brought a new governor, Jacob A.O. Preuss, to replace Joseph A.A. Burnquist in the Minnesota statehouse. In Washington, Warren Harding, who called for a return to "normalcy," replaced Woodrow Wilson at the White House.

Eventually, the scars left by the First World War would heal. The German mottos in the state capital would be restored and the controversies and conflicts that marked that earlier era would fade away into history. Now, as the 100th anniversary of America's first Great War approaches, it is time to rediscover an important, complex and difficult episode in this state's history.

Prologue

SUMMER DAYS 1914

As July gave way to August in 1914, thermometer readings inched up toward ninety degrees. With a midsummer heat wave settling over the Twin Cities, throngs of city dwellers cooled off with a trip to the beach. For many in Minneapolis, that trip meant a short drive to the chain of lakes on the city's west side.

"Bathing suit clad pedestrians may be seen in the lakeside districts…at almost any hour," the *Minneapolis Tribune* reported. "The bathing suit habit has extended even to those living many blocks from the lake and fortunate to own an automobile," the paper noted. "The sight of a machine filled with bathing-suit clad people is almost as common today as are the machines, themselves."[3]

Across the river in St. Paul, the trip to the beach took a little longer. That city's large aquatic playground, White Bear Lake, was about twelve miles north of St. Paul's downtown.

At White Bear, "Swimming takes on a bohemian air," observed the *St. Paul Pioneer Press*. "Those who have cottages on the lake run down to the shore almost unseen. Those who live a block or so away, go back and forth clad in bathrobes or only in bathing costumes.[4]

That weekend, the heat wave did not deter baseball fans who sat in the sun at Nicollet Park, watching the Minneapolis Millers come from behind to defeat the Cleveland Bearcats five to four. The Minneapolis team had been trailing Cleveland until the ninth inning, when Fred Hunter's single drove in two winning runs for the Millers.

A summer heat wave drew throngs of Minneapolis residents to the city beaches in July 1914 at the outbreak of World War I. *Courtesy of Hennepin County Public Library Special Collections.*

Twin Citians who were looking for indoor entertainment during the first weekend in August had many options. They could choose from the shows at more than eighty theaters and vaudeville houses scattered throughout the two cities. The Sunday afternoon matinee at the Metropolitan featured Paul J. Rainey's newest African hunt motion picture. "Rainey's movie brought the wildest part of Africa to Minneapolis," the Metropolitan declared in its weekend ad.

On their way to the beach, the ball game and the theater during that summer weekend, many Twin Citians might not have paid much attention to the front-page news that two countries in southern Europe were at war. Unless they followed the twist and turns of international politics, these Minnesotans were probably not aware of the web of international treaties that would soon escalate this regional conflict into a worldwide military calamity.

In Minneapolis, some local businessmen did pay close attention to the article on the front page of the *Minneapolis Journal* just under the headline that Austria had declared war on Serbia. That article reported on the rapid rise in wheat futures.

THE MINNEAPOLIS JOURNAL.

AUSTRIAN GOVERNMENT DECLARES WAR ON SERVIA; BELGRADE REPORTED TAKEN BY INVADING FORCES

LIQUOR INTERESTS AND POLICE ON TRIAL IN CHICAGO VICE WAR

End of Reign of "Hinky Dink" and "Bathhouse" Johnas Kings of the Levee Seen.

TODAY'S WAR DEVELOPMENTS

Austrian government sends formal notification of declaration of war to Servia.

Austrian troops reported to have crossed the Danube, seized Belgrade and begun northern invasion of Servia.

Two Servian steamers seized at Orsova on the Danube by the Austrians, Servian flag hauled down and Austrian colors hoisted.

Efforts of great powers, it is assured, will be exerted today localizing area of hostilities.

WHEAT SOARS AS WAR NEWS COMES TO MINNEAPOLIS

September Option Bonds Up 7 Cents Today on Chamber of Commerce.

Hostilities Are Formally Opened After Rejection Of Mediation Proposals

The *Minneapolis Journal* reported on the rapid rise in wheat futures just as news about the Austrian war declaration reached Minnesota. *Public domain.*

Grain traders knew the war would drive up the demand and the price for flour at home and abroad. In Minneapolis, then the world's flour milling capital, wheat futures were always a local preoccupation. Here, the price of wheat had a more direct impact than the fighting in far-off Europe.

Across the river in St. Paul, the war was getting front-page headlines, but that city's leaders had more immediate concerns. They were frustrated by the lack of progress in rebuilding St. Paul's railroad hub, the Union Depot, destroyed by a fire in 1913.

Following the fire, railroad passengers in St. Paul had to make do with a makeshift facility on the site of the old terminal. Now that war had started in Europe, railroad officials were preparing for a rapid increase in traffic through the temporary station, when many foreign nationals, now living in the state, decided to return to their native countries.

SUPPORTING THE HOMELANDS

In St. Paul, with an estimated population of fifty thousand Germans, Austrians and Hungarians, leaders of the three ethnic communities began organizing a mass meeting to demonstrate a show of support for their European homelands. Planning for the meeting began on August 2. That day, Edgard Prochnik, the Austro-Hungarian consul in St. Paul, announced that a general mobilization of the entire Austrian army had just been ordered. The mobilization meant that all men living in the United States with Austrian military obligations were required to return home and report for active duty. In Prochnik's consular district, which included Minnesota, the Dakotas and parts of Wisconsin and Michigan, about twelve thousand Austrian nationals were affected by the mobilization order.

"I want the men to go back as soon as possible," Prochnik said. "But I do not want them to be idle in New York or come to St. Paul and be idle here. As soon as I learn that transport is available, men will be asked to assemble here and sent east."[5]

The next day, Germany's consul in St. Paul, H.E. Grunow, reported that the German army and navy had been mobilized. The mobilization order required German reservists to ready themselves for military duty. Grunow estimated that only about two hundred men living in St. Paul were covered by the German government's decree.

Later that week, St. Paul's mayor Winn Powers issued a proclamation calling for St. Paulites to maintain harmonious relations with one another even while their family members in Europe were on opposite sides of the escalating European conflict

"A terrible war the ravages of which cannot be comprehended is threatening Europe, involving many nations," Powers declared. "In this city, we number among our citizens natives of all the nations of the world. It is inevitable that sympathies of our adopted sons should be with the country of their nativity in times like this."[6]

STRANDED IN THE WAR ZONE

Aside from the Germans, Austrians and other foreign nationals who faced the prospect of military duty back in their home country, only a handful of Minnesotans were directly affected by the newly declared war.

That handful consisted of a few local residents who were stranded in Europe as the troops began to mobilize. They included Mrs. L.M. Hall and her daughter, Gertrude, a music student in Berlin. In August, their Minneapolis relatives reported that Mrs. Hall and her daughter had not been heard from for over a month, since the outbreak of war in July. Local businessman Charles Lewis was quite concerned about his niece, Georgia Kober, who had also been a music student in Germany. Lewis appealed to the U.S. State Department for news about his niece, who had been in Berlin when the war began and had lost contact with her family in Minnesota.

Friends and family members were reassured when they learned that several University of Minnesota medical school instructors who had been traveling in Europe were able to book passage back to the United States on a steamship sailing from Liverpool on August 18. As a result of transatlantic travel delays, University president George Vincent was faced with the unexpected need to fill a number of staff vacancies on a temporary basis. He had recently learned that several of his faculty members, still traveling in Europe, would not arrive back in Minnesota for the start of the new college term in September.

A Lighthearted View

With the war still nothing more than a front-page curiosity for most of its readers, the *Minneapolis Journal* was able to take a light-hearted look at the escalating overseas conflict. In early August, the paper quoted some fictional "celluloid collar strategists" who were arguing among themselves about events in Europe. "That Kaiser Wilhelm is a bluff and a false alarm and has been all over Europe throwing a scare in people," said the big man. "But now his bluff is called, and they are going to use him as a rag to wipe Germany off the map." Then, the little man bounded forward. "You are a nice big stiff you are," he shouted. "A guy goes in and take on five guys for a fight, and you want to see the same guy licked do you? You want to see five guys jump on one guy and beat him up, do you? You are a sport, you are, ain't you?"[7]

Even young people were getting war fever, according to the *Journal*. "War is a game among Minneapolis youngsters," the paper reported later in the month. "Military cocked hats fashioned out of newspaper are bobbing about at the corner lots. The toy drum has been hauled forth from the attic arsenal and giving up lusty sounds to the distraction of non-combatants."

"It has been impossible to keep a broom in the house lately," declared a North Minneapolis mother. "My son and his playmates insist on using them as muskets. If these depredations don't stop, I am going to issue a declaration of neutrality and back it up with a slipper."[8]

The *Journal* took a lighthearted view of the war, when it was nothing more than a front-page curiosity for most of its readers. *Public domain*.

FOES CLOSER TO HOME

Youngsters living in the southern Minnesota farming communities may have found time to play war games, but mainly they were kept busy helping their parents with the endless round of midsummer chores.

During the early days of August, as armies mobilized in Europe, many Minnesota farm families were facing a foe closer to home. That week, the *St.*

Peter Herald noted that hog cholera was on the rise in the surrounding county. The paper reported that the St. Peter Commercial Club "had enlisted with the forces that are fighting the spread of the disease."[9]

In that same issue, the *Herald* profiled William Kohl, a local resident who had served in the German army during the short lived Prussian-Danish War. Kohl was a member of the German regiment that marched into Denmark in February 1864. At the battle of Eckenforde, he was wounded in the right knee by a piece of shrapnel that tore through his saddlebag. The former German soldier still carries the scar from that wound, the *Herald* reported. "He has no difficulty recalling the wounds and the suffering on the battlefields of Denmark, and those recollections make him an earnest advocate of peace," the paper noted.[10]

Not to be outdone by Kohl, another St. Peter resident, Andrew Kopp, reported that he, too, had been a member of the German army. Kopp had fought in Franco-Prussian War of 1870 and came through a series of battles unscathed. "He still glories in the triumph of the German arms and regrets that he is not now in a position to march with legions of the Kaiser," the *Herald* told its readers.[11]

Kopp could not have known it at the time, but in just a few years, his regrets about not marching with the Kaiser would be considered treasonous in his adopted hometown of St. Peter.

THUNDERCLOUDS

An overflow crowd jammed into the Minneapolis Auditorium and spilled out into the street on the evening of September 22, 1914. The crowd had assembled there to demonstrate its support for U.S. neutrality as an escalating military conflict was underway across the Atlantic.

In its account of the 1914 event, the *Minneapolis Tribune* reported that Minneapolis had joined a "World Peace Army."[12]

The organizers of the neutrality rally had taken their cues from President Woodrow Wilson. A month earlier, the president had issued a statement calling on his fellow countrymen to remain "impartial in thought as well as in action." Wilson acknowledged that many Americans might want to choose sides in the European war, because so many had ties to the nations that were now combatants. But such actions "might seriously stand in the way of proper performance of our duties as the one great nation at peace," he declared.

At the Minneapolis Auditorium on September 22, University of Minnesota president George Vincent echoed the president's words. Vincent urged the crowd not to be neutral for "selfish self-protection, but because of the opportunity it presents for America to play her part in making war impossible. In this way, we may help in building world peace."

Albert Allen, one of the rally's organizers, made an impassioned plea to his enthusiastic audience. "God has put us in a country of peace," Allen declared. "We, too, have a war party that tells us we must mount the same horse they are riding in Europe. We are met here in this meeting that you and I can be prepared to meet that argument when it is presented to us." Allen went on to note that the Upper Midwest, with its large influx of newly arrived immigrants, was filled with people who had strong ties to the countries that were at war with each other in Europe. "Here we are brothers, neighbors. Across the sea they are fighting," he declared. "We should act so as not to disturb the feeling of brotherhood."[13]

In its editorial later in the week, the *Tribune* provided the statistics to bolster Allen's case. The paper reported that Minnesota's population included 400,000 Germans, 130,000 Englishmen, 70,000 Austrians and 30,000 Russians. "In America, these folks are neighbors to each other and to us," the paper noted, echoing Allen's words. "In Europe, they are engaged in a bloody conflict. We must guard against imperiling their relationships, here in a land of peace and freedom."[14]

The next month, on October 11, churches in the southern Minnesota town of New Ulm were filled with worshippers who had come to celebrate "Peace Sunday." At the First Congregational Church, the morning sermon was delivered by Mr. F.W. Johnson, who declared, "The one great lesson that America must learn from this death dance of the nations in Europe is that military preparedness is not a guarantee of peace but an absolute guarantee of war." At the nearby St. Paul's Lutheran Church, that Sunday's collection was earmarked for Lutheran congregations in Germany.

Conflicting Views

On Peace Sunday, the people of New Ulm learned that their highly respected mayor, Dr. L.A. Fritsche, was returning home after a three-month trip to Europe. Later that week, when Fritsche arrived at the town's train station he was met by a brass band and a crowd of more than two hundred well-wishers. The crowd was composed primarily of German Americans, who reflected the ethnicity of New Ulm and the surrounding communities.

Fritsche, himself the son of German immigrants, had visited Berlin after war had been declared. The mayor reassured his neighbors that conditions in the German capital were quite normal. Only the occasional troop movements indicated that a military conflict was underway, he reported.

New Ulm's leading citizen said he was convinced that war was "thrust upon" Germany and not instigated by it. For this reason, he said, "the German people are united as never before and there is absolutely no doubt in their minds that victory will be theirs." To back up his contention that Germany was the victim rather than the instigator of the war, Fritsche claimed that French troops, threatening Germany, had actually crossed the border into Belgium before war was declared.[15]

In the Twin Cities, the early days of the war were viewed quite differently. There, the local papers portrayed Germany as the aggressor that had invaded defenseless Belgium. By the end of August, war bulletins published in many U.S. papers had a clear pro-Allied slant. The mainstream press, including the *New York Times*, carried a provocative report from a Belgian commission then in London. According to the *Times*, a commission spokesman described the war as "a return to savagery" with his people being used as slave labor by the Germans. "It is what was done in the Middle Ages," the spokesman added angrily.

In its coverage of the commission, the *Times* signaled its clear support for the Belgian position. The paper observed that, while Belgium was not planning to ask for direct U.S. support, in view of the American declaration of neutrality, "there is a secret hope that when the American people learn the full truth about what has happened in Belgium there will be a spontaneous outburst of indignation which may bring some definite results." [16]

In Minneapolis, besieged Belgium became a cause célèbre, as reports about worsening conditions there received front-page coverage in the local papers. In November, the wife of the Belgium ambassador, Madame Lechtervelde, received an enthusiastic reception when she came to town to raise funds for Belgium relief.

Her visit coincided with a joint effort launched by the city's leading flour milling companies, to provide food aid for the Belgians. The local firms announced that they were sending a cargo of flour to "help feed the women, children and old men of Belgium rendered destitute by the war."[17]

FADING NEUTRALITY

In 1915, as the war in Europe dragged on with no end in sight, mainstream public opinion in the U.S. began moving steadily away from a policy of neutrality. That move accelerated when the British ocean liner the *Lusitania* was sunk by a German U-boat on May 7, 1915. The naval action came after Germany posted warnings in U.S. papers that the ship was a target of attack because it was carrying British armaments. A Minneapolis resident,

George Arthur, was one of the 128 Americans on board the *Lusitania* who were killed when the ocean liner was torpedoed. Arthur, a twenty-eight-year-old machinist, was on his way back to his home in England to work in a munitions plant.

In an effort to tamp down growing U.S. indignation over the *Lusitania* incident, President Wilson called for restraint in a speech to fifteen thousand people in Philadelphia's Convention Hall. "America must be an example of peace," Wilson declared, "not merely because it will not fight, but of peace because peace is the healing and elevating influence of the world, and strife is not."

Then, in a phrase that received widespread attention, he observed, "There is such a thing as a man who is too proud to fight. There is such a thing as a nation being so right that it does not need to convince others by force that it is right."[18]

Immediately, Wilson's political opponents jumped on the phrase "too proud to fight" and used it as club to attack him. Noting that 128 American had been killed by the German attack, Senate Republican Leader Henry Cabot Lodge declared that "it was not the time for fine words or false idealism…The phrase 'too proud to fight' uttered at such a moment, shocked me as it did many others."

Former president Theodore Roosevelt, a fierce war hawk and one of Wilson's bitterest foes, called for immediate U.S. military action to avenge the sinking of the *Lusitania.* "We as a nation earn measureless scorn and contempt if we follow the lead of those who exalt peace above righteousness, if we heed the voices of those feeble folk who bleat to high heavens that there is peace when there is no peace," Roosevelt thundered.[19]

In Minnesota, the sinking of the British ship elicited a broad range of responses. The *Minneapolis Journal* condemned the German naval attack in harsh terms but avoided any call for an American response. "The sinking of the *Lusitania* shows that Germany intends to outdo the barbarians and become the outlaw of nations," the *Journal* declared angrily. "War is horrible enough, cruel enough, savage enough when carried out in accordance with civilized rules. But without rules without a sense of humanity…war may be made like hell incarnate. It looks like this is Germany's conception of war."[20]

Former University of Minnesota president Cyrus Northrop, then head of the Minnesota Peace Society, sounded a note of calm detachment when he observed, "The Lusitania was a British ship. Germany is at war with Britain. It has given warning that it would sink the British vessel, and it has done so, and that is all there is to it."[21]

William Watts Folwell, Northrop's predecessor as university president, was somewhat more disturbed by Germany's aggressive action in the North Atlantic. "The right to sink freighters has been conceded, but with passenger vessels, the case seems doubtful," Folwell noted. "The action is outrageous, anyhow. It doesn't tend to bring the war to a close."[22]

Roosevelt and the war hawks kept beating the war drums following the *Lusitania* sinking, but Wilson resisted the call to arms. In its editorial, the *Minneapolis Tribune* voiced its support for the president, saying that he "has dealt with the difficulties confronting him so well thus far, that we are encouraged to think that he will meet the new situation wisely."[23]

Top: Cyrus Northrop, the head of the Minnesota Peace Society, sounded a note of calm detachment when he commented on the sinking of the *Lusitania*. *Courtesy of the Minnesota Historical Society*.

Right: William Watts Folwell called the German naval action "outrageous" but doubted that it would hasten the end of the war. *Courtesy of the Minnesota Historical Society*.

IMAGING THE BATTLE ZONE IN MINNESOTA

The Somme offensive, one of the bloodiest battles of the war, occurred during the summer and fall of 1916. When the offensive ended, the British and French forces had made only minimal progress in pushing back the German front line.

In this excerpt from its October 29 edition, the *Minneapolis Journal* imagined that the Somme battle zone had been transposed to Minneapolis:

> *Suppose for the moment that Nicollet Island was fortified with all the skill of modern military engineering. Suppose again that an attack force was entrenched in a half circle extending from Twenty Sixth and Emerson Avenue North, its line crossing Twentieth Avenue North and Loring Park. Would you think it would take the attaching army very long to reach Nicollet Island, granted that it was superior in men and artillery?*
>
> *It took the French and British army from August 26 to September 26 to traverse exactly that distance in the Somme offensive and the allied generals complimented their troops enthusiastically.*

HE KEPT US OUT OF WAR

By 1916, as the war became entangled with domestic politics during a presidential election year, Wilson's Republican critics kept arguing that the president, now a candidate for a second four-year term, was not dealing with the situation in Europe wisely.

In October, former Indiana senator Albert Beveridge came to Minnesota to rally support for the Republican presidential candidate Charles Evans Hughes. In a speech at the Minneapolis auditorium, Beveridge mocked the Democrat's slogan that "he [Wilson] had kept us out of war." Their slogan "is no more an argument in [Wilson's] favor than to say that the administration should be kept in power because the president did not burn the White House," the Indiana Republican told the crowd of enthusiastic Hughes supporters.[24]

As the election grew closer, the Republican and Democratic presidential campaigns ran dueling ads in the Twin Cities' daily papers. The campaign rhetoric was shrill in both political camps. For their part, the Democrats tried to tie Hughes to Roosevelt, the country's most prominent hawk, claiming that the choice was between "Wilson and Peace with Honor" or "Hughes with Roosevelt and War."

"Roosevelt says we should hang our heads in shame because we are not at war with Germany on behalf of Belgium!" the ad read. "Roosevelt says that following the sinking of the *Lusitania* he would have forgone diplomacy and seized every ship in our ports flying the German flag. That would have meant war. Those who place the almighty dollar ahead of human life would not hesitate to plunge this country into an ignoble war of conquest—would not stop at sacrificing thousands of American lives in their greed for oil and gold."[25]

In its ad, the Republican National Committee asked rhetorically, "Has he kept us out of war?" The RNC answered its own question, claiming that

Woodrow Wilson campaigned for reelection in 1916 as the peace candidate, as shown in this newspaper cutout. *Public domain.*

the Democrats' slogan was false. "We have been at war," the committee maintained, referring to the U.S. army's skirmishes with the Mexican revolutionary Poncho Villa at the U.S. Mexican border. "We are now at war, many lives have been lost; our honor has been besmirched. The fact is that he [Wilson] has neglected our greatest treasures—the lives of our citizens and the honor of our country."[26]

On election day, November 7, 1916, the election was closer in Minnesota than any of the political prognosticators could have predicted. Wilson and Hughes were virtually tied in this state. Hughes's microscopic margin of 392 popular votes swung Minnesota's 12 electoral votes to the Republican candidate, who ended up losing to Wilson in the Electoral College by 23 votes.

A RAGING CAMPUS STORM

In the spring of 1917, as war with Germany seemed increasingly likely, Minnesota was no longer marching in the "World Peace Army" as it had done three years earlier. As war fever mounted, even the term "peace" became a dirty word. In March, a group of Macalester College students found themselves in the eye of a raging political storm because they had the temerity to express their views about the fast-changing international events. The students, members of the college Neutrality and Peace Association, had drafted a resolution urging support for what was, at that point, Wilson's policy of "armed neutrality."

Duluth congressman Clarence R. Miller responded to the resolution with a blistering attack on the college peace group. "You call yourselves neutral; you are not," Miller thundered. "You are pro-enemy and anti-American. You say you are for peace, but you say it under circumstances that surrenders America and Americans to their enemies."

The Duluth congressman went on to imply that the students were cowardly and "yellow streaked" and were "welching" when confronted with their duty to support their country."[27] Miller succeeded in cowing a number of the male students who now regretted they had signed the resolution when they found that they were being tarred as cowards. One Macalester freshman, Morris Finstad, told the *St. Paul Pioneer Press* that he had signed the peace resolution but he didn't know what he was signing. "Someone is always passing around resolutions and a fellow has to sign for friendship," Finstead explained, making excuses for his earlier errant action. The college freshman said he was enlisting in the naval militia to show that he was not a coward and that he was "for America first, last and always."[28]

Finstead was not the only person on campus who had an abrupt change of heart. Macalester professor James Wallace, who had been vice-president of the Minnesota branch of the American Peace Society, announced that he was resigning from the peace organization because he no longer believed in its cause.

Wallace had become an ardent supporter of the war and now maintained that advocating for peace was unpatriotic. One chronicler of the Macalester incident explained that Wallace and those who shared his views invoked "a sense of national manhood" in their advocacy for war. Opposing U.S. involvement

Macalester professor James Wallace became an ardent hawk once war was declared. *Courtesy of the Macalester College Archives.*

in the war, they believed, was a sign of weakness and cowardice. "With the support for the war cast in these terms, the manhood of men who supported neutrality was brought into question."[29]

PATRIOTIC FRENZY

Almost overnight, many Minnesota doves, like Wallace, turned into hawks when Woodrow Wilson urged Congress to declare war on Germany. His congressional message included the often quoted phrase that war was needed "to make the world safe for democracy." The edition of the *Minneapolis Tribune* that carried the announcement of Wilson's message also included a report that a Minneapolis man, Adolf Hendrickson, was aboard the U.S. merchant ship *Aztec* when it was struck by a German torpedo. Hendrickson was one of twenty-eight men aboard the ship, who were missing and

First Armed U. S. Ship Sunk, Minneapolis Man Aboard

The Minneapolis Morning Tribune

MINNEAPOLIS, MINN., TUESDAY, APRIL 3, 1917

Wilson Asks State of War Declaration and 500,000 More Soldiers for Army

A Minneapolis seaman was aboard a U.S. merchant ship when it was sunk by a German torpedo just as the United States was preparing to go to war in support of its European allies. *Public domain.*

presumed dead when the ship was sunk off the coast of France. The *Aztec* was the first merchant ship carrying the U.S. flag that was armed to protect it from German attack.[30]

The approach of war unleashed a patriotic frenzy all across the country. That frenzy was on display in Minneapolis at an emotional prowar rally on April 6. Three years earlier the *Minneapolis Tribune* had reported on another widely attended event where Minneapolis had enlisted in the "World Peace Army." Now the citizens at this latest gathering were "smoldering volcanoes of patriotism," according to the *Tribune*, "as the call to arms was greeted with wild cheers and standing ovations."

The rally, held at the West Hotel, provided a platform for a series of speakers, including former secretary of war Henry L. Stimson and F.C. Walcott, a Wall Street banker who had arranged U.S. loans to Britain and France. Walcott maintained that Germans, intent on occupying Belgium, planned to round up all able-bodied Belgians and ship them to Germany, where they would be forced to work in German industrial plants.

The New York banker was followed at the speaker's platform by a Mr. Coudert, who was not identified by his occupation or first name. Coudert told the crowd that there were only "two classes of people in America today—Americans and traitors." He claimed that the "German system has told its people that Americans have only one ideal, gold. It said we would not fight because we were cowardly and because we would not want to give up our horde of wealth. It misunderstands us just as it misunderstood the little Belgian nation."[31]

At the West Hotel rally, one local political figure was conspicuous by his absence. Minneapolis's Fifth District congressman Ernest Lundeen was in Washington voting against Wilson's war resolution. Lundeen was joined by three of his Minnesota congressional colleagues and more than forty other

U.S. House members who opposed the congressional action authorizing a declaration of war. Following his vote, the war's supporters, including the *Minneapolis Tribune*, heaped scorn and abuse on Lundeen, who maintained that his own poll of constituents showed a lack of support for the war.

In a news article, with a headline that read, "Lundeen Condemned by Constituents," the *Tribune* declared that "Minneapolis was woefully misrepresented in Congress when Ernest Lundeen voted against the resolution declaring a state of war. That was the opinion that was addressed on all sides yesterday." If there were constituents who supported Lundeen, the *Tribune* made no effort to seek them out.[32]

Lundeen was still not back in his home district on April 19 when eight thousand Minneapolitans marched down Nicollet Avenue in a parade marking the 142nd anniversary of the Battle of Lexington and Concord, which launched the Revolutionary War. One of the most prominent participants in the April march was eighty-year-old Maria Sanford, one of the best-known women of her day in Minnesota. Sanford had been one of the first women to serve on the faculty of the University of Minnesota and had made a name for herself as a champion of women's rights and women's suffrage. During the march, she jumped from the automobile in which she had been riding and onto an army wagon, later she told the cheering crowd, "Those like myself who can't do the fighting must give our last dollar and our last ounce of strength to uphold the arms of the men who are doing the fighting. The country relies on all of us to maintain its honor."[33]

While Minnesota's mainstream press was encouraging the prowar fervor, there were some dissenting views expressed in the state's labor papers. In his April 6

Minnesota's Fifth District congressman, Ernest Lundeen, was roundly criticized for his vote against the congressional war resolution. *Courtesy of the Minnesota Historical Society*.

Eighty-year-old Maria Sanford was a prominent participant in a prowar rally on April 19. *Courtesy of the Minnesota Historical Society.*

editorial, the *Minneapolis Labor Review*'s outspoken editor Robley Cramer cast a critical eye at the frenzy surrounding the march toward war. "Is it any wonder there is a strong pacific sentiment in this country," Cramer observed, "when it is possible to hear on a public conveyance in this town, a group of expensively dressed and slimy souled creatures talking about war as a good thing for business." Then, in a more restrained statement, Cramer observed that "patriotism is, of course, love of land and race. But is true patriotism manifested in blind devotion to such utterances as 'my country right or wrong? We think not."[34]

2

GEARING UP

In April, soon after Congress declared war, local leaders turned their attention to homefront preparedness. "While young manhood is getting khaki ready to do the actual fighting the rest of the community is organizing to stand back of the boys with home, defense, organizations of material, first aid and other preparedness measures," the *Minneapolis Tribune* noted, just days after the war declaration was issued in Washington.[35]

Along fraternity row at the University of Minnesota, "young manhood" was getting ready to do its part to aid the war effort. Soon after word reached Minnesota that war had been declared on April 6, men began pouring out of the fraternity houses along University Avenue, cheering and singing "The Star Spangled Banner" as they marched down the street four abreast. Similar demonstrations were springing up on college campuses all across the country.

In 1917, many young Americans viewed war as a romantic adventure where men could demonstrate their bravery and manliness while upholding the honor of their country. Three years earlier, a similar wave of romanticism had taken hold in Britain. That country's "best educated and talented young men rushed willy nilly to the colors, and, just as quickly, to die in the mud of Flanders" observed Stanford historian David Kennedy.[36]

On Minnesota campuses, "the best educated and the talented" rushed to enlist even before registration for a newly authorized military draft began in June.

QUESTION

HOW CAN I HELP MY COUNTRY?

ANSWER

I'll Fight—
> Be a Volunteer in Uncle Sam's Army or the Home Guards.

I'll Farm—
> The War is one of Wheat, Corn and Potatoes as well as Soldiers and Firearms. Men must eat.

I'll Give—
> The worst SLACKER is the man who is not only willing to let others face Bullets on the Battlefield, but refuses to give.

I'll Invest—
> Buy Uncle Sam's Bonds. Bonds are better than tax receipts. Better Bonds than Bondage.

I'll Conserve—
> Plan to avoid Waste, particularly of Staples. Cut out extravagance of Dress and Diet.

Above: "While young manhood is getting khaki ready to do the actual fighting, the rest of the community is organizing to back up the boys," the *Minneapolis Tribune* declared just days after war was declared.

Left: Homefront preparedness became a preoccupation for local community leaders soon after the United States entered the war. *Courtesy of the Minnesota Historical Society.*

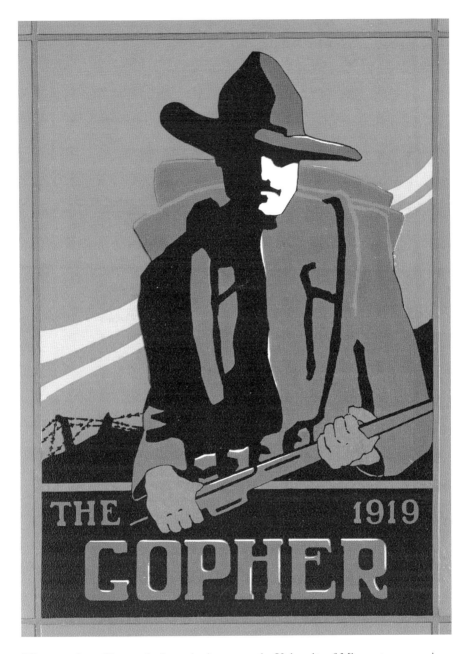

This page and next: The war had a major impact on the University of Minnesota campus in 1917 and 1918. These images from the university's 1919 yearbook provide a commentary on campus life during those years. *Courtesy of the University of Minnesota Archives.*

A GRIM SHADOW, cast by a darkening cloud, lies upon our campus. ¶ The storm center is still distant, yet we feel the tremors of the world shaken by this time of travail. ¶ The old is being tried; the new awaits its birth. ¶ The call for succor has come and we have not been found wanting. ¶ From our best have gone our challengers. ¶ They have borne with them the fires of a holy purpose. ¶ Their returning shall not be with lowered standards nor with craven compromise. ¶ Let them not find in us the selfsame spirit of yesterday, which tho conscious of this world purification has failed to remove its own dross. ¶ Better that they die in battle, on purified soil, than to return but to find that our ideals were for our neighbors only.

COMPELLING TO SERVE

Legislation establishing the draft and the Selective Service System had been approved by Congress and signed into law by President Wilson earlier in the year, after a certain amount of political maneuvering by both branches of government.

As the Selective Service bill moved through Congress, there was substantial jockeying over a provision inserted in the legislation by Republican lawmakers to permit fifty-eight-year-old "Colonel" Theodore Roosevelt to raise his own division to fight in France. Roosevelt's independent action would have been a huge source of embarrassment to

The cartoonist Frank King used his weekly cartoons to support draft registration. *Public domain.*

the Wilson administration, which succeeded in eliminating the provision as a mandatory requirement in the bill.

In Minneapolis, registration day, June 6, became a quasi-holiday when the city's saloons and many of its stores were closed. All men between the ages of twenty-one and thirty were required to register for the draft unless they were already serving in the military.

Frank King, who later created the popular series *Gasoline Alley*, devoted his weekly cartoons in early June to draft registration and enlistment. Through the year, King would use his drawing to generate support for the war effort in a lighthearted way.

In early June, the *Tribune* provided the list of questions that the men would be expected to answer when they appeared at the registration centers. One asked registrants to state whether they had a family member who was solely dependent on them for support. "Consider your answer carefully," the paper cautioned. "If it is true there is another mouth other than your own, which you alone have a duty to feed, do not let your military order interfere with the wish of the Nation to reduce the war's misery to a minimum. On the other hand, unless the person you have in mind is SOLELY dependent on you, do not hide behind petticoats or children."[37]

Hennepin County sheriff Otto Langum signaled his uneasiness about the military preparedness event when he summoned five hundred special deputies to serve during the registration day. Langum's apprehension may have stemmed from his fears that a recent draft riot in Chicago might provoke a similar disturbance in Minneapolis. At the end of May, Chicago police had broken up a socialist antiwar demonstration and began attacking and arresting many of the two thousand who had attended the rally.

"I look for no particular trouble but if it comes, we will be prepared to meet any contingency," Langum declared, after rumors began to circulate that the socialists might try to disrupt the registration process in Minnesota.[38] By the end of registration day, Langum found there was little need for his huge crew of special deputies. Few, if any, incidents occurred at the state's numerous registration sites. A total of nearly forty thousand men had registered for the draft in Minneapolis, with only a handful refusing to register on moral or political grounds. Two of them, twenty-two-year-old Robert Skoglund and his twenty-one-year-old brother, claimed they were socialists and were jailed for their act of defiance. In St. Paul, four men refused to register because they claimed the forced conscription violated the Thirteenth Amendment to the United States, which prohibited involuntary servitude.

The Skoglund brothers and the four St. Paulites represented a tiny minority of draft-age men in Minnesota, almost all of whom acquiesced to the draft even if they did not embrace it enthusiastically. At the university, many of its young men were enthused about their new opportunities for military service. Some had gotten the jump on the draft by volunteering for officers training at nearby Fort Snelling.

GEARING UP

THE NEW LEADERS

Minnesota's historic fort, established in 1819 at the confluence of the Mississippi and Minnesota Rivers, had been hurriedly pressed into service during World War I when the War Department realized that it was woefully understaffed with junior officers. Thousands of new second lieutenants and captains were needed for a rapidly ballooning military force expected to reach the level of a half million men in troop strength.

At Fort Snelling the first of two training camps was set up to turn out junior officers after an intensive three-month training program. Candidates were required to provide recommendations from community leaders when they appeared at the enrollment stations, hoping to obtain one of the nearly 1,900 training slots reserved for civilians from the states in the Upper Midwest. When the University of Minnesota's station opened in the campus armory on April 23, the armory's halls "were packed with three hundred eager, jostling young men lined up to turn in their applications," according to one observer.[39]

Military officials expressed some concern that the training program was attracting the very young—the fraternity boys who marched down University Avenue—rather than the more seasoned and mature community leaders who could have provided the leadership skills that the army needed. Those seasoned and mature leaders might have been reluctant to sign up for officers training because they probably realized that the war was not going to be the lark that the fraternity boys hoped it would be.

The first group of officer candidates arrived at Fort Snelling on the morning of May 11. After a physical exam, the young men were assigned to a barracks and received the olive drab uniforms they would wear during their three-month training program. Reveille was sounded at 5:15 in the morning and the lights were not off until 11:00 p.m., so the young men put in an intensive and exhausting eighteen-hour day during their weeks at Fort Snelling. The first five weeks of the program were devoted to classroom instruction on the fundamentals of military science while the remaining eight weeks were devoted to combat training. The men were able to obtain leave on the weekends from Saturday noon until Sunday night. But leave could be withheld for minor infractions of the rules like carrying a dirty rifle or stepping out of line at drill.

The officer candidates soon learned that schoolboy pranks had no place at their training camp. One night, when a training officer was making an inspection of the barracks, he discovered that one of the men seemed to

This page: Young men from the Midwest were able to receive their commissions as junior officers after undergoing an intensive three-month training regimen at Fort Snelling. *Courtesy of the Minnesota Historical Society*.

be lying in his bunk in a peculiar position. The officer check the bunk and discovered that a dummy figure stuffed with pillow was under the blanket. When the young man who had set up the dummy returned from his night on the town, he was arrested and summarily dismissed from the camp the next morning.

During the eight weeks of combat training, several skirmishes were fought on the bluff across from the Fort on the Mendota side of the Minnesota River. These were the "battles of Pilot Knob." The men were ferried

Minnesota's National Guard units expanded their ranks to meet the war's manpower needs in 1917 and 1918. *Courtesy of the Minnesota Historical Society.*

THE BEST MELTING POT IN THE WORLD

In late May, the *Minneapolis Tribune* published what it said was a first-person account of the training experiences of one unnamed Minnesota infantry recruit. The recruit wrote,

> *Three weeks ago, four of us, strangers to each other, enlisted in the First Minnesota Infantry. One of us was a sturdy Scandinavian lumberjack, another was a son of a rich man, the third was an irresponsible youth who had never possessed a home, another five years out of college had left an office job to join the army. You should see us lined up now, and you couldn't tell who was who, for the American army is the best melting pot in the world. We feel already that we are almost soldiers, although we know that weeks and months of drilling are ahead of us before we are efficient. But our olive drabs feel comfortable on us now. We carry our Springfield rifles with grace, and our muscles are beginning to stiffen for the trials ahead.*[40]

Many of the Minnesotans who signed up for duty in the state's national guard units found themselves shipped off to Camp Cody, a training center in a desolate stretch of New Mexico. One observer

Above and opposite: The armed services employed skilled artists to create arresting recruitment posters. *Public domain*.

described the unfamiliar scene that confronted the newly minted soldiers from the Upper Midwest when they stepped off the train at the hastily constructed training camp. "They saw a vast sandy waste, upon which was appearing a mushroom growth…long rows of wooden mess halls facing streets that seemed to stretch away interminably; innumerable rows of tents…and gray, dusty patches of mesquite and yucca in spaces ultimately to be cleared for drill grounds."[41]

Minnesota draftees were often able to take their training closer to home, at Camp Dodge, a five-thousand-acre training camp ten miles north of Des Moines Iowa. With the outbreak of war, the U.S. Army quickly went to work ballooning the size of the camp, which had served as the home of the Iowa National Guard. Construction crews worked around the clock, building enough barracks to house the thousands of men getting trained at the Iowa camp.

While facilities at Camp Dodge and the other training centers were primitive at best, trainees with some off-duty

These draftees from Duluth probably received their basic training at Camp Dodge in Iowa. *Courtesy of the Katherine A. Martin Archives at the University of Minnesota–Duluth.*

Once they completed basic training, Duluth soldiers on home leave could show off their uniforms to hometown admirers. *Courtesy of the Katherine A. Martin Archives at the University of Minnesota–Duluth.*

This event was raising funds to support the YWCA's Hostess Houses, which provided a respite for soldiers in the U.S. training camps. *Courtesy of the Hennepin County Public Library Special Collections.*

hours could find a few touches of home at the sprawling camps known as cantonments. The camps were equipped with athletic fields, recreation centers and movie theaters. Many of the camps also had specially designated buildings known as Hostess Houses, where soldiers could meet with their mothers, wives and girlfriends in a homelike setting. The Hostess Houses were operated by the YWCA, one of the many local and national service organizations that provided homefront support for the troops in 1917 and '18.

across the river and then marched up the steep bluff in full battle gear and ninety-degree summer heat to the top of the bluff, where the skirmishes between opposing units occurred. On the second day of the climactic two-day battle, the men maneuvered back to the fort against an imaginary enemy line that forced them to shield themselves in a series of trenches that they dug themselves. This phase of the training was intended to prepare them for the trench warfare that was the hallmark of World War I.

One sympathetic observer of the training scene wrote that "morale was high…muscles were hardened and hands calloused. Instead of the fatigue felt at the close of the early hikes, the men enjoyed high spirits and laughed and sang familiar marching songs as they stomped back to camp."[42]

The officer's training camp at Fort Snelling was not the only military training underway in Minnesota in 1917. The 151st Field Artillery, a unit of the state national guard that was placed under federal control during World War I, conducted its own training for its recruits near Fort Snelling. The 151st was one of the many regional and national military units that mounted aggressive recruiting campaigns as the war got underway.

In Washington, the major service units hired the country's top graphic artists to create dramatic and compelling recruitment posters. The most famous poster of the period, now a widely recognized iconic image, was created by James Montgomery Flagg. It shows a stern-looking Uncle Sam pointing his finger at a potential recruit and telling him, in a threatening tone, "I want you for the U.S. Army."

FINANCING THE GREAT CRUSADE

While the draftees and volunteers were preparing to go "over there" to join their British and French counterparts on the western front, Minnesotans who remained at home were able to do their part to support the war by purchasing U.S. Treasury obligations known as liberty bonds.

As early as 1916, when the Wilson administration began ramping up military preparedness, administration officials knew they needed to generate a substantial increase in revenues to fund a huge expansion of federal activity. In Washington, ballooning cost projections led to a debate in Congress over whether to generate revenues by taxation or by borrowing. Three years earlier, in 1913, the Sixteenth Amendment to the Constitution had taken effect, authorizing a federal income tax. Now, reformers in Congress wanted to expand the income tax, in part to make it more progressive but also to blunt the growing preparedness movement.

Understandably enough, big-business interests resisted the move for higher taxes and opted instead for borrowing. In Minnesota, the *Union Advocate*, the editorial voice of the Minnesota Federation of Labor, slammed the Minnesota Manufacturers Association, the state's business lobby, in an April 1917 editorial. The *Advocate* maintained that the business group was "opposed to direct taxation and in favor of a bond issue because it was determined to shift the burden from its own shoulders to those of the workers of the contemporary and future generations."

With an even harsher tone, laced with sarcasm, the labor paper observed that "it is not expected that any of them [members of the association] will enlist for service on the battlefield. Their lives are too precious and their services at the munitions plants are too valuable to be risked where men fall by the thousands in death dealing conflicts of opposing armies. Only common workingmen are proper persons to face such hazards. But the government needs an immense amount of money and surely these manufacturers ought to be willing to contribute generously to this branch of service from which the wealth they have coined out of the blood and agony of the soldiers and their suffering families in Europe."[43]

Wilson tilted toward the progressive, pro-tax position and was able to win some limited increase in taxation, but his secretary of treasury, William McAdoo, believed the federal government needed to rely primarily on borrowing to fund the war effort.

In April 1917, McAdoo proposed a $2 billion bond issue to fund the war, which was substantially higher than most of Wall Street had expected. McAdoo realized that a conventional borrowing at that level could disrupt the country's capital markets, so he devised a plan to sell the first issue of the bonds, with a below-market interest rate of 3.5 percent, to the general public rather than to Wall Street investors. McAdoo's marketing stroke of genius was to convert federal borrowing into a national crusade to support the war effort. Now, it was every American's patriotic duty to buy the federal bonds.

"We went directly to the people," McAdoo was later quoted as saying. "And that meant to everyone—to businessmen, workmen, farmers, bankers, millionaires, school-teachers, laborers. We capitalized on the profound impulse called patriotism. It is the quality of coherence that holds the nation together; it is one of the deepest and most powerful of human motives."[44]

The result was one of the most effective and far-reaching marketing efforts ever conducted by the federal government up to that time. Charles Dana Gibson and other well-known illustrators were hired to produce arresting and highly propagandistic posters to sell Liberty Bonds. For the first time, entertainment celebrities like Douglas Fairbanks and Mary Pickford were also enlisted in the cause.

In Minnesota, community leaders and local editorialists quickly jumped on the liberty bond bandwagon. Here, the Ninth Federal Reserve District, headquartered in Minneapolis, oversaw the bond sale. An elaborate

Prominent American illustrators created colorful posters designed to promote the sale of liberty bonds.

hierarchical structure was established with layers of committees at the local, county and state levels reporting up the ranks to the overall Ninth District chairman, a Minneapolis businessman, Arthur R. Roberts. Soon virtually every editorial outlet in Minnesota was voicing support for the liberty bond crusade. These included several German-language newspapers whose editors wanted to demonstrate their support for the war and deflect the anti-German sentiment that was building in many of their communities. Even the *Minnesota Union Advocate*, which had argued for a federal tax increase to fund the war rather than a bond sale, came out in full support for the liberty bond campaign.

THE WAR BUSINESS

Minnesotans may have been asked to sacrifice financially and personally to support the war effort, but there were economic benefits, as well, flowing into the state as local industries geared up to meet the rapidly rising need for raw materials, equipment and supplies. In Minneapolis and St. Paul, local businessmen eagerly sought war-related federal contracts. A number of them were successful—particularly those whose companies manufactured clothing and bedding. One of the largest local suppliers, the North Star Woolen Mill, was located on the downtown Minneapolis riverfront. It received a contract to produce 100,000 blankets at a price of $6.50 per blanket. In St. Paul, two footwear firms received $200,000 in orders to produce thirty-five thousand pairs of army shoes. One local observer noted that "everything considered, northwestern firms equipped to handle government contracts received their fair share of the war business, although the smaller establishments were generally out of the running, because their capacity for production was too small to give them recognition."[45]

Duluth, with its strategic location at the head of the Great Lakes, emerged as a major shipbuilding center. Three local shipbuilders—McDougall-Duluth, Superior and Globe—employed more than five thousand workers during their period of peak production in the fall of 1918. During the war years, McDougall-Duluth, the largest of the three companies, manufactured thirty-five seagoing vessels, each designed to pass through the Welland Canal, connecting Lake Ontario with Lake Erie.[46]

Much of the iron ore used to build the Duluth ships came from nearby Mesabi Iron Range, which covered an eighty-mile stretch of northern

SHIPBUILDERS!

It is the patriotic duty of every workman who is not already engaged in an essential enterprise to secure employment that is essential.

THE McDOUGALL-DULUTH CO.
SHIPBUILDERS

REQUIRE IMMEDIATELY

SEVERAL HUNDRED

Skilled and unskilled able-bodied men for work in their shipyards at once!

WHY GO ELSEWHERE?

"DO IT FOR DULUTH" AND DEMOCRACY.

—APPLY—

United States Employment Service
301 West Michigan Street, Duluth

This page: The Duluth shipyards had a major impact on the region's economy during the war years. *Courtesy of the Katherine A. Martin Archives at the University of Minnesota–Duluth.*

Minnesota. The range saw a huge increase in the demand for its iron ore as U.S. industrial activity spiked during the war years. In 1916, the mining district had been the site of a bloody strike by workers who succeeded in shutting down the mines for two months. The strike had been organized by the fiercely militant International Workers of the World. With a wave of hyper-loyalism sweeping through Minnesota in 1917 and 1918, the IWW would become the target of those who equated the union's organizing activities with a treasonous mission to sabotage the war effort.[47]

THE LOYALTY CRUSADE

With war frenzy mounting day by day during the late winter and early spring of 1917, it was only a matter of time before that frenzy worked its way into political maneuvering at the state capitol.

In the Twin Cities, organizations sprang up to generate public support for the approaching war. The St. Paul group was known as the Patriotic League while the Minneapolis organization identified itself as the Liberty League. At the urging of both groups, the legislature adopted a measure requiring local school boards to display an American flag in every school in their districts. Soon, the leagues were doing more than flag waving. They were raising the specter of sabotage by the Wobblies, who had a strong base of support in northern Minnesota. At the same time, the prowar leagues were eyeing the state's German American communities suspiciously. New Ulm, in southern Minnesota, was a major target because of the widespread support there for American neutrality.[48]

In the closing weeks of the 1917 legislative session, the prowar leagues began ramping up public support for legislative efforts to suppress the IWW and place aliens under public surveillance. To deal with these supposed threats, many of the loyalists wanted to give state government broad new powers to move against any actions viewed as disrupting public order during a time of war.

UNCHECKED POWERS

At the end of March, legislation began moving through the house and senate to create a new state agency that came to be known as the Minnesota Commission of Public Safety. The seven-member commission would be composed of the current governor, J.A.A. Burnquist; the attorney general; and five members to be appointed by Burnquist. While an early provision calling for the registration of aliens was stripped from the final version of the bill, the commission was given virtually unchecked powers to suspend civil and political liberties during wartime. These powers included the authority to remove local elected officials from public office if their loyalties were suspect. Legislation establishing the commission was signed into law by Governor Burnquist on April 22, 1917, two weeks after the U.S. Congress declared war on Germany.

The language authorizing the commission declared that it "shall do and perform all acts and things necessary and proper so that the military, civil and industrial resources of the state may be most efficiently applied towards the maintenance of the defense of the state and nation and towards the successful prosecution of such war."[49] Eventually, the commission would push its authority beyond the words of the statute to suppress legitimate union organizing and ban political meetings by leftist groups that were suspected of disloyalty. In his history of the commission, Carl Chrislock noted that the agency's actions were theoretically subject to judicial review but that judges were reluctant to question the legality of those actions given the public fervor about the war. Chrislock quoted William Watts Folwell, a historian and former president of the University of Minnesota who observed that "if a large hostile army had landed at Duluth and was about to march on the capital, a more liberal dictatorship could hardly have been conceded to the Commission."[50]

Burnquist, the commission's champion and now a fervent war hawk, had been a staunch progressive when he was first elected to the Minnesota House at the age of twenty-nine. In 1912, he retained his Republican label even though he supported Teddy Roosevelt's unsuccessful third-party bid to oust the incumbent Republican president, William Howard Taft. In 1914, Burnquist was elected lieutenant governor and moved up to the state's top office when the incumbent governor, Winfred Hammond, died in office in 1915.

The St. Paul Republican, elected governor in his own right in 1916, delivered a strongly progressive address when he was inaugurated for a full term in January 1917. Burnquist called for women's suffrage, expanded state public health efforts and an overhaul of the state's child labor laws.

A St. Paul reporter termed the address "the most progressive message any governor has handed out yet."[51]

Yet like many progressives of that era, Burnquist had no difficulty reconciling his reformist views with a full-throated support for the war. By law, the governor was designated chair of the Commission of Public Safety, but Burnquist ceded leadership to the agency's most extreme and outspoken member, John F. McGee. During the agency's brief but tumultuous two-year life, McGee was clearly the commission's driving force.

McGee was a corporate lawyer from Illinois who had grown up in an Irish immigrant family. In 1887, after practicing law for a time in North Dakota, McGee moved to Minneapolis, where he quickly rose in the city's legal ranks, becoming a full-fledged member of the local political and social establishment. Unlike other Irish Americans who were noninterventionists during the early years of the war, McGee was a staunch supporter of the Allied cause. Like many intense partisans, McGee was rock solid in his beliefs. He once declared, "I have no doubt whatever that I am right and knowing that I am right there is no power on earth that can budge me one inch from following the path of duty as I see it."[52]

McGee's duty as he saw it was to root out any vestiges of dissent about the war. His position as the commission's most forceful member gave him the power and authority to pursue his cause. According to Carl Chrislock, McGee "saw the commission as an opportunity to suppress not only out-and-out pro-German sentiment but also trade unionists (whether moderate or radical) members of the Nonpartisan League, socialists, pacifists and all who entertained the slightest doubt with respect to the wisdom of America going to war."[53]

As the commission bill moved through the legislature, McGee, who was well connected in state Republican circles, lobbied for a post on what would soon be a powerful new state agency. He made no secret of his extremist views when he declared, obviously referring to himself, "If the Governor appoints men who have backbone, treason will not be talked on the streets of this city and the street corner orators, who denounce the government, advocate revolution, advocate against enlistment, will be looking through the barbed fences of an internment camp out on the prairie somewhere."[54]

When the commission was organized at the end of April, McGee was assigned the key position of overseeing the Minnesota Home Guard, a local militia organized to take the place of the Minnesota National Guard that had been federalized for the duration of the war. Through the spring and summer of 1917, McGee, as the commission's most active member, turned his full attention

Above: The Commission of Public Safety took an expansive view of its powers to maintain public order. *Courtesy of the Minnesota Historical Society.*

Left: John McGee, emerged as the real power on the Public Safety Commission. *Courtesy of the Minnesota Historical Society.*

to organizing the home guard, a quasi-military organization intended to supplement the public safety efforts undertaken by local police departments. Because the draft and military recruitment by the U.S. armed services was underway, the home guard needed to draw its manpower from able-bodied men over thirty-one, the age limit for the draft, or between the ages of twenty-six and thirty-one if the prospective guard member, though physically fit, had been exempted from the draft for some reason.

Due in large part to McGee's efforts, the home guard rapidly expanded during the war years. By April 15, one year after the commission was established, the guard had reached a force level of 350 officers and more than 7,000 enlisted men. Under McGee's direction, the guard's job was to maintain order and deal forcefully with any group or individual intent on disrupting the peace. In the summer and fall of 1917, the guard would carry out that role during the bitter strike by workers at the Twin City Rapid Transit Company.

TARGETING HYPHENATED AMERICANS

Even while a labor-management conflict was building at the transit company, the Safety Commission was keeping a watchful eye on developments in the heavily German American town of New Ulm in southern Minnesota. New Ulm was established in 1854 by a group of German immigrants from the province of Württemberg in Germany. The town was named for Ulm, the major town in that German province. During the Dakota war of 1862, New Ulm was attacked by Dakota warriors who killed a number of townspeople. The Dakota war would remain an important part of New Ulm history, as the town continued to celebrate its German heritage and culture in the years leading up to World War I.

In the summer of 1917, John McGee's suspicions about the German Americans in New Ulm were heightened when he learned about a rally there dealing with the draft. The July 25 event, which attracted a crowd of nearly eight thousand to New Ulm's Turner Park, was one of southern Minnesota's largest gatherings, according to the *New Ulm Review*. "If any came expecting to hear the government unjustly or severely criticized, they were doomed to disappointment," the *Review* observed.[55]

New Ulm mayor Louis Fritsche, speaking from a platform decorated with bunting and American flags, sounded a somber note when he delivered

New Ulm took pride in its German American heritage. *Courtesy of the Minnesota Historical Society.*

opening remarks at the conclave. As reported in the *Review*, Fritsche told the crowd that the rally "was intended to be a peaceable gathering of American citizens, who had come together to petition Congress, not to send into war any Americans soldiers, except those who would go voluntarily…There was absolutely no desire on the part of [the rally organizers] to cause any dissatisfaction with the existing draft law but that, on the contrary, the law would be explained and upheld, and only proper, peaceable and legal means would be discussed about bringing about the desired result."

At the July rally in New Ulm, Albert Pfaender, the New Ulm city attorney, delivered the main address. Pfaender began by recounting the service of German Americans in the Civil War and the Spanish-American War, where their loyalty to the United States was clearly demonstrated. In the current war, they were prepared to do their duty, but many were troubled by the overseas conflict, he maintained.

"This nation by the judgment of its Congress, duly elected by the people, is at war with a foreign nation," Pfaender told the largely German American audience. "This gathering of American citizens realizes the fact more than those who are instrumental in bringing about this condition. For the burden of war falls upon the average common citizen and not on those who sit in cushioned chairs in the white walled palaces of our nation's capital."

"As one of the measures for carrying on this war," Pfaender continued, "Congress has passed the so-called draft law under which the drawing has just taken place to determine the order in which those liable to military duty shall respond to the call. It is the consequence of this call, which has brought about a spirit of inquiry and uneasiness among people reflected in this meeting tonight."

In his address, Pfaender did question the legal underpinnings for the military draft then in place. He acknowledged the U.S. government's constitutional authority to establish military conscription in order to repel an invasion, but he believed the Constitution did not authorize a draft to create a U.S. army to fight in an overseas war.

Despite his misgivings about the draft, New Ulm's city attorney urged the young men in his audience who had been drafted to obey, according to the *New Ulm Review*'s account of the rally. "He declared it to be the duty of those young men to respond promptly when called," the paper reported. "'Nothing can be gained by resisting the draft,' he said. At the same time, he said it is up to those who remain at home to use every honorable means in their power to bring about a constitutional amendment providing for a constitutional amendment providing for a referendum on the question of war."[56]

In the following days, word of the New Ulm rally spread throughout the state. One local newspaper editor, the *Princeton Union*'s Robert Dunn, initially took a light-hearted view of the event. On July 26, he wrote, "New Ulm, Brown County, where English is hardly ever spoken, is figuratively up in arms against the United States government, and wants to secede from Minnesota and the Union and declare itself a 'Free City of Germany.' It would be too bad if we should lose New Ulm, for it is a pretty little city, manufactures a fine grade of beer and some mighty nice people live there."[57] Later in the summer, Dunn's humor had evaporated when he issued a vitriolic attack on the southern Minnesota town, noting that "there are those who regret that the Sioux did not do a better job at New Ulm fifty-five years ago."[58]

The New Ulm rally did strike a responsive chord in several of the state's other German American communities, where similar events were being planned. "Seditious meetings are being held with impunity all over Minnesota," Dunn reported in his Princeton paper. "The Copperheads [antiwar Democrats during the Civil War] are rampant."

THE ULTIMATE SANCTION

With editorial writers like Dunn inflaming loyalist passions, the Safety Commission decided that it needed to move against the New Ulm men who had organized the July 25 rally. The commission had laid the groundwork for an investigation when the agency directed Fritsche and other New Ulm officials to appear before it. Ambrose Tighe, the commission's legal counsel, laid out the case for the commission's action when he wrote that local officials like Fritche and Pfaender were expected to ensure compliance with all properly enacted statutes. "For such officials to publicly throw discredit on existing laws is inconsistent with the obligations they have assumed and exposes them to charges of malfeasance."[59]

Even before the order was implemented, Pfaender offered to appear before the commission to lay out the concerns of his fellow New Ulm officeholders. In an effort to diffuse the situation, the city attorney invited the commission to send its representative to his town to monitor local meetings about the war and to insert a restraining hand in the proceedings if it looked as if the meetings were getting out of control. McGee and the other commissioners rejected Pfaender's invitation and proposed instead that he, Fritsche and a third local official, Henry Berg, sign a pledge promising to cooperate the with the commission. When the three men refused to sign the pledge, the watchdog agency moved to remove the three from office. At its August 22 meeting, the commission adopted a resolution calling on Governor Burnquist to take that step. The next day, Burnquist complied, and three men were stripped of their posts.

The *New Ulm Review* gave scant attention to Burnquist's action, noting merely that Mayor Fritsche, City Attorney Pfaender and County Auditor L.G. Vogel had been "suspended from office because the Commission wanted it." The *Review* went on to report that "the governor designated William Packer as Mr. Vogel's successor and W.D. Eibner as temporary mayor. However, he has failed to notify either of them of their appointment. All they know about it is what they have read in the papers. In the meantime, New Ulm is not sure it has a mayor and Brown County is in doubt about its auditor."[60]

In an editorial earlier in the month entitled "What Is Misconduct?" the *Review* observed that Albert Pfaender, a retired army officer, "told the men who had been drafted that the government was acting wholly within its right; that Congress had a perfect right to pass the draft laws, and that it was the duty of every drafted man to respond." The *Review* went on to report that the Minnesota Bar Association, following the July 25 event, had adopted a resolution introduced by "an upstart lawyer" from Mankato demanding the disbarment of Major Pfaender on grounds of misconduct. "In Heaven's name, what is misconduct?" the *Review* asked with a tone of exasperation. "Will the Mankato upstart kindly inform an anxious public?"[61]

Then, the New Ulm paper vented its feelings about what it saw as the injustices suffered by its community:

> *Certainly, there never was greater need for men, real men, thinkers who can stop in the midst of passion and prejudice that are rife just now, to give a clear and unbiased decision when it comes to matters of patriotism. Here we have in Minnesota a tyranny more absolute than anyone dreamed could possibly exist in free America and yet in the blindness of prejudice induced by war hysteria, who can see clearly that it is tyranny that is being practiced every day? Few indeed except those directly affected by the tyranny. And yet justice demands that even those who are not affected by the stringent rulings of the Safety Commission should stand up for the rights of those put down by those rulings. It cannot possibly be fair to prohibit anti-draft meetings so long as loyalty meetings are allowed. One set of ideas has as much right to be given publicity as the other set. Nobody in New Ulm protests against the holding of loyalty meetings by those whose inclinations run that way, but the loyalists have secured a ruling that no more peace meetings can be held. What justice is there in such a conduct of affairs? How long can we barefacedly call this "Free America"?*[62]

The *Review* found little editorial support for its anguished views, but at least one local newspaper did express some sympathy for the tribulations facing the German American communities in southern Minnesota. The *Martin County Independent*, published in the nearby town of Fairmont, noted that the German people are

> *among the best, most thrifty, industrious, useful and law abiding part of our population and yet there are many in Fairmont and elsewhere who delight in hurling insults and bitter insinuations and charges against them. The German people of Martin County and elsewhere are not responsible for the crimes of the despotic tyrant across the sea nor the Prussian military system which is a curse to the people of the Fatherland and menace to the world.*
>
> *The great majority of them are loyal to Old Glory. It is for them a trying time. We are at war with their Fatherland...Many of them have dear relatives fighting with our enemies. Their hearts bleed and their souls are tried, but not a moan is heard. There are Germans in this country who are*

At the recommendation of the Public Safety Commission, Governor Burnquist removed New Ulm mayor L.A. Fritsche (left) and city attorney Albert Pfaender (right) from their elected posts. *Courtesy of the Brown County Historical Society.*

giving their sons to fight their brothers across the sea, and yet they utter not a word of complaint. But, in spite of their loyalty they must bear the insults hurled at them by craven cowards.[63]

STRUGGLE IN THE STREETS

While events were playing out in southern Minnesota, the Twin Cities would soon become the center of another wartime controversy. There, Horace Lowry, the head of the Twin Cities Rapid Transit Company, was embroiled in an escalating dispute with his employees. Lowry's company, founded by his father, Thomas, in 1890, operated the streetcar system in Minneapolis and St. Paul under a franchise agreement with both cities.

In 1917, TCRT employees, dissatisfied with wages that had not kept pace with inflation, petitioned Lowry for a three-cent-an-hour raise. When he refused, claiming that the company could not afford the increase, they decided to form a union. To help them organize, the TCRT workers approached a national labor organization, the Amalgamated Association of Street and Electric Railway Employees. The national organization responded by sending its organizers to the Twin Cities. Soon, the labor group began making headway by signing up members for two new union locals, one in Minneapolis and the other in St. Paul. Lowry responded by promptly firing the union's leaders. At the same time, he maneuvered to buy off the remaining TCRT employees by offering them a 10 percent pay wage increase. Flexing their muscles, the two new Amalgamated locals rebuffed Lowry and called on his workers to strike the transit company.

The strike began at 1:00 a.m. on October 6. In Minneapolis, the strike was relatively peaceful with only a few episodes of violence reported, but the situation was quite different in St. Paul. There, thousands of strikers took control of the streets and shut down virtually all streetcar service. The next day, the *St. Paul Pioneer Press*, aghast at the events unfolding around it, reported that "wild rioting in which the police were unable to control mobs numbering in the thousands marked the end of the first day of the strike."[64]

With the labor action spinning out of control, Governor Burnquist called on U.S. Army officials at Fort Snelling to send in federal troops to quell the disturbance. Soon, five hundred infantrymen were patrolling the streets of St. Paul, armed with bayonets and rifles. This show of force caused the strikers to back off, permitting TCRT to resume normal streetcar service in both cities. Army patrols may have quelled the labor riot in St. Paul, but the bitter dispute, which provoked the street violence, remained unresolved.

The next day, in an effort to settle the dispute, the Public Safety Commission intervened with a directive that generated support from both sides—at least initially. Drawing on its legislative mandate to suppress civil unrest during wartime, the commission ordered an immediate end to the strike. Then, in an effort to appear evenhanded, the state agency also called for review of management's discharge of the fifty-seven workers. The *Minneapolis Labor Review* reacted somewhat prematurely by declaring that "Street Railway Strike Ends in Victory for Men."[65]

TCRT employees did receive a pay raise and most of the men fired by Lowry at the onset of the strike were reinstated. But, as the weeks wore on, union supporters found that their initial gains were beginning to erode. On the defensive, Lowry set out to create his own company union, known as the Trainmen's Co-operative and Protective Association. TCRT's owner appointed himself head of the new organization, with the ultimate authority to resolve any dispute submitted by its membership.

As a sign of their support, Protective Association members were issued blue buttons to wear on their caps. Almost immediately, the Amalgamated locals responded by issuing yellow buttons for their supporters. Now, the "war of the buttons" had begun. Lowry's blue buttons proved to be a tactical blunder. Pro- and anti-union trainmen were clearly identified by the buttons on their caps. Some passengers who were union sympathizers began spitting on their nickel fares or throwing their nickel on the floor when they encountered a blue-buttoned conductor as they boarded their streetcar.

The Amalgamated Union, having some faith in the commission's impartiality, called on the agency to intervene in the labor dispute again. In response to the request, the commission appointed a three-member committee to investigate and present its recommendation back to the full seven-member body. The committee's report, issued on November 19, called for all union solicitation to cease on company property and for all employees to cease wearing the buttons that identified them as pro- or anti-union.

Once again, the Public Safety Commission intervened, this time issuing an order on November 20 banning the display of buttons or other insignia by the streetcar motormen. The commission's order, as it applied to union organizing, was somewhat ambiguous. It merely declared that "this is not a convenient time for agitation about abstract principles like Unionism or non-Unionism." Immediately, Lowry moved to implement the commission ruling by directing all his employees to remove their buttons.

Events moved quickly as union officials began preparing for a mass meeting of their membership to determine their next steps in face of the commission ruling. On November 26, Lowry further inflamed union passions by issuing a provocative order declaring that any employee displaying a button on company property would be immediately fired.

A week later, on Sunday, December 2, angry workers withstood plunging temperatures at an outdoor meeting in St. Paul's Rice Park. Some speakers at the mass event called for restraint as the labor controversy neared another crisis point, but the rank and file were in no mood to heed that advice. Once again, as they had done in October, union members went on a rampage as the meeting was breaking up, attacking nearby company supporters and halting streetcar service.

"At least 2500 persons quickly gathered at Seventh and Wabasha, most of the crowd coming from the union meeting at Rice Park," the *Pioneer Press* reported. "Cries of scab were heard as the street cars with difficulty made their way through the packed streets. Then someone threw a brick through the window of a car on Wabasha Street and the pent up energy of the rioters broke loose."[66]

This time, Governor Burnquist responded to the violence by mobilizing the Minnesota Home Guard. Within a few days, calm returned to the streets

The Minnesota Home Guard patrolled the streets of downtown St. Paul following a violent rampage by angry workers in December. *Courtesy of the Minnesota Historical Society.*

as the state troops marched up and down Wabasha and St. Peter Streets and the city's other major downtown thoroughfares. The St. Paul streets might have been calm, but the dispute between the streetcar workers and the TCRT management continued to simmer. By now, the Public Safety Commission was signaling its support for Lowry and his effort to beat back union organizing efforts among his workers.

During the months of the wartime strike, the relationship between Minnesota's labor movement and the commission pointed out the tensions between various factions in the movement. The more moderate leaders of the Minnesota Federation of Labor did what they could to deflect charges that labor in Minnesota was disloyal. Several of the leaders cooperated with the commission, although they continued to voice concerns that labor was not represented on the state agency. At the federation's state conference in April, the commission was the subject of a heated argument between the labor organization's moderates and its militant wing. The militants maintained that the commission was in league with the state's big employers, who were using the issue of loyalty to suppress labor organizing. The militants introduced a resolution calling for a special session of the legislature to abolish "this unnecessary and menacing State Safety Commission." The resolution was defeated by a vote of 228 to 72, but a later motion to commend Governor Burnquist and the commission was also defeated.[67]

As it looked back at the strike a year later, the umbrella group representing St. Paul labor, the Trades and Labor Assembly, was still smoldering with anger about the events of 1917. In a report entitled "The Truth About the Street Car Trouble," the group condemned the actions of its management foes—"designing men," in its words, acting to further "their own selfish purposes, in a way to bring about a state of affairs that is seriously injurious to this community." The St. Paul labor group maintained that the strikers were merely exercising "their constitutional rights as free American citizens to organize a union for the protection and promotion of their interests as working men."

The union group was particularly irate about the role of the Safety Commission, a state agency that had been viewed by some labor leaders, at least initially, as an impartial arbiter. "The law [creating the commission] went through on a wave of patriotism and most people believed that Gov. Burnquist would select a representative commission that could administer the great power bestowed on it for the welfare of the whole population," the Labor Assembly noted. "The people were disillusioned, however, when the governor made his selections. The workers and farmers of Minnesota constitute 80% of the state's population. Yet neither a farmer nor a labor representative was named on the public safety commission. Instead, it [the commission] was made up of men notorious for their hostility to organized labor."

To bolster its case, the St. Paul labor group pointed to the commission orders that, the group said, backed Lowry in his dispute with his workers. "This unjust and arbitrary procedure of the state safety commission was taken as an indication that the commission was determined to uphold the streetcar company in whatever course it chose to pursue in dealing with its employees, and this conviction brought on the second street car disturbance."[68]

The Public Safety Commission and its allies in Minnesota did achieve some short-term victories in 1917 and '18. But in some ways, it won the battle but lost the war. By incurring the wrath of rural interests represented by the Non-Partisan League as well as the urban interests represented by transit workers and other militant unions, the commission served as a common enemy for the two left-leaning political movements that hadn't always shared common interests. This link helped create a foundation for Minnesota's Farmer Labor Party, which would become the dominant force in Minnesota politics during the early years of the Great Depression.

LIFE ON THE HOMEFRONT

In the late winter and spring of 1918, the war was not going well for the western allies. In early March, the eastern front collapsed when the newly installed communist government in Russia laid down its arms and signed a peace treaty with Germany at Brest Litovsk. Then, later in the month, the Kaiser's forces launched an offensive along a fifty-mile stretch of the western front, pushing the besieged British and Canadian troops back toward the English Channel. But help was on its way as the newly trained American Expeditionary Forces, under the command of General John J. "Black Jack" Pershing arrived in France and rushed to the front.

By the spring of 1918, the United States had been a combatant for nearly a year, but the full impact of the war was just now being felt in Minnesota. The state's 151st Field Artillery, a Minnesota National Guard unit, now federalized as part of the Pershing's Rainbow Division, had only just reached the front lines. On March 4, the 151st suffered its first battlefield casualty when Sergeant Theodore Peterson was killed in a skirmish with Germans near the town of Badonviller in northern France.

Later, Private Clare West, with the Field Artillery's Battery D, would write home about his experiences on the battlefield during that early skirmish. West told about being gassed and waking up in a military hospital, unable to see. But then, as the effects of the gas wore off, he was able to regain his sight. "We had received our orders to take our positions for our first experience in battle," West wrote from the hospital where he was convalescing. "Strange as it seems to me now, I was not one bit nervous, nor was I frightened. I had taken up my position in front, preparing for the big order when suddenly the Germans let go. About eight shells showered the ground about my feet…Well, for a few minutes, I was startled and then I got mad. We got our order to put on our gas masks and got busy just then, and for six hours, we gave the Germans all they were looking for. Quite a few of us got it, but not until we had handed the Huns a shower."[69]

While West was recuperating in an army hospital, reports reached Minnesota about the British army's evacuation of the town of Armentieres in the face of the German assault. The town was left in ruins as British troops retreated toward the North Sea coast.

WHIPPING THE KAISER

Back in Minnesota, homefront preparedness and support for the war had become a daily preoccupation for local civic leaders, who did what they could to maintain morale in the face of disturbing reports from overseas. In early April, the *Minneapolis Journal* reported that twenty-five thousand Minneapolitans would be marching in a loyalty parade through downtown Minneapolis. The parade would serve as the kickoff of the local campaign to raise funds to "whip the Kaiser," the *Journal* announced. The Minneapolis campaign was part of a nationwide effort to generate sales for the newly authorized Third Liberty Loan, intended to generate an additional $3 billion in bonds to finance the war. "Minneapolis is to have a Liberty Bell that will ring out its deep notes, and Minneapolis will witness the biggest parade in its history," the *Journal* declared with a note of pride.[70]

Across the river, St. Paulites were planning to launch their own Liberty Loan campaign with a pageant at the city's auditorium. The *Pioneer Press* advised its readers to sign up early for the pageant tickets because they were going fast. Ticket sales got a boost from a local military leader, Colonel A.L. Parmeter, the head of Fort Snelling's Thirty-sixth Infantry. Parmeter noted that the St. Paul event was coming just as the German offensive was underway on the western front. "It [the pageant] will help bring home to our people here as nothing else can do the realization that we are in this war to a conclusive finish and that it can and will end only one way—victory for American arms," Parmeter declared. "Those of you at home have not even the faintest idea of the real life of our boys over there. Could you know one tenth of the sacrifice they make for you, could you realize even a little of the

Duluth civic groups mobilized to promote the sale of liberty bonds and stamps in 1918.
Courtesy of the Minnesota Historical Society.

trials they undergo, cheerfully, earnestly, enthusiastically, I am convinced the Third Liberty Loan would be an insignificant task."[71]

As the German offensive continued in the spring of 1918, towns all across Minnesota geared up to support the Third Liberty Loan. In Duluth, community leaders coordinated bond sales with the sales of War Savings Stamps. While the bonds were sold in denominations starting at fifty dollars, a single stamp could be purchased for twenty-five cents. "Personally, I am going to put all the money I can into Liberty Bonds," George C. Stone, the head of Duluth's bond campaign, told the *Duluth News Tribune*. "After I have done that, I am going to put the money I can't spare into war stamps. In case of doubt, I think every American ought to dig up until he has to say 'ouch.'"[72]

In Mankato, community leaders launched their liberty loan campaign at an April 11 rally. North Dakota chief justice Andrew Bruce was the guest speaker at the campaign kickoff, held at the Mankato Theater. Bruce's career had been "a source of inspiration to young men, especially those of foreign birth who have come to the shores of this country to carve out their fortune," the *Mankato Daily Free Press* reported.[73]

In the nearby town of Amboy, German-born Fredrick Osten-Sacken addressed a bond rally on April 4. At the rally, Osten-Sacken told his Minnesota neighbors that he had returned to Germany for a visit in 1913 after an absence of thirty years and was distressed by what he found there. "The leaders have no more regard for the people than they have for cattle and use them as so much cannon fodder," the German-born Minnesotan declared. "America is in this war for self-protection, for the Kaiser has said,

'I have dreamed of world domination and by my mailed fist will bring it about.'" Osten-Sacken told his enthusiastic audience, "We are in this war because every ideal of America is hated by kaiserdom, and would be crushed out if Germany is victorious."[74]

In St. Paul, a group of Minnesotans with German ancestry took steps to distance themselves from "kaiserdom" by organizing a League of Patriotic Americans of German Origin. In its bylaws, the organization stated, "We hereby pledge our unswerving support and loyalty to all war authorities and the military activities that our glorious country is engaged in, for the absolute purpose of winning the war." In an address to the league's organizing convention, E.G. Quamme, president of the Minnesota Farm Loan Bank, told the members of the newly formed organization that they "must seek out every man of German origin and ask him to prove his loyalty. Or if you find him disloyal, insist that he no longer call himself a German American. He is a German and you should inform the authorities who he is and where he lives."[75]

In Minneapolis, the rhetoric was even more heated at the rally launching the city's Liberty Day Parade. Frank Odell, a representative of U.S. Treasury secretary McAdoo, told the crowd, "We want only liberty and we will have it when we drive the Hun back to hell from whence he came with his rule of baby killing and frightfulness. All he has is the poison gas borrowed from the sulphurous fumes of hell and the liquid fire from the savages of old."[76]

These soldiers from Windom were part of a force of more than forty thousand Minnesotans serving in the U.S. armed services one year after America entered the war. *Courtesy of the Minnesota Historical Society.*

A broad cross-section of Duluth residents, including these chorus girls from the Empress Theater, supported the war effort. *Courtesy of the Katherine A. Martin Archives at the University of Minnesota–Duluth.*

The *St. Paul Pioneer Press* took a more restrained approach in a full-page ad on April 6 marking the one-year anniversary of the U.S. declaration of war. With unconcealed pride, the paper noted that the anniversary "finds St. Paul, its citizens and business organizations with an enviable record. Its great business houses and factories have contributed liberally of their best manhood, their equipment and resources and yet are speeding their work up to the highest efficiency of their country's call." The paper reported that sixty-two of its own employees were serving in the U.S. military.[77]

One year into the war, 41,000 Minnesotans were serving in various branches of the armed forces, according to Major John Snyder with the Minnesota Adjutant General's Office. Of that number, 14,000 were army enlistees and just under 18,000 were draftees. Snyder predicted that over 100,000 Minnesotans would be in the service by the end of the year. In fact, that goal would be met, even though the war would end much quicker than Snyder and other local military officials might have predicted in the spring of 1918.

WAR CONSCIOUSNESS

In the spring of 1918, war consciousness seemed to permeate daily life in Minnesota. For days on end, reports from the battlefield filled the front pages of the local papers. During those weeks, the overseas military struggle even found its way into the sports pages, where the *Pioneer Press*'s Robert Ripley reminded his readers:

> *American athletic history is replete with instances where indomitable courage and pluck resulted in ninth inning rallies which changed defeat into victory. Hard pressed as they are, the Allies' spirit and the Allies' line are still unbroken…The courage and unconquerable souls of France, England and America will survive the hardest blow and plunge forward again with a will undying, and victory, like the dawn, will shatter the darkness and radiate towards heaven.*[78]

With the military conflict "over there" a daily preoccupation for many Minnesotans, local businesses were not above using the war as a marketing tool in their newspaper ads. The Standard Clothing House in downtown Minneapolis declared, "The war is making men practical. Styles are plainer—more military."[79] Down the street on Nicollet Avenue, the Maurice L. Rothschild Company told its customers, "For good boys' clothes, look to us. Military modes, of course, lead all others. Real olive drab materials in suits of Uncle Sam services styles, Jr. Pershing models. As for sailor—regulation long pants." In its ad, Powers Department Store wrapped itself in the flag, at least figuratively, when it declared, "One year ago, America declared war on the enemies of democracy. The Stars and Stripes is the emblem for which we fight." The store went on to advertise cotton flags ranging in price from ten to seventy-five cents, and wool bunting flags measuring three by five feet for six dollars.[80]

As Minnesotans noted the one year anniversary of the U.S. declaration of war, the Strand Theater announced that it soon would be showing *The Kaiser—the Beast of Berlin*. In breathless prose, the theater declared that the new film "strips naked the soul of history's maddest murder king!" The Strand warned "alien enemies [to] keep away! This picture is not for you. **KEEP AWAY** from this theater unless you wish to be maddened by the exposé of the Kaiser's rotten **KULTUR**. This is the story of the bloody beast who seeks to make the world German—who seeks to destroy all that blocks his insane purposes."[81]

The U.S. film industry, then in its early years, made highly propagandistic movies during the war. This ad promoted a movie playing at the Strand in downtown Minneapolis. *Public domain.*

In his Sunday sermon on that same weekend, Reverend Ambrose Bailey, pastor of St. Paul's First Baptist Church, matched the Strand Theater with his invective aimed at the Kaiser. Bailey told his congregation that the German monarch was "the supreme example of the embodiment in human flesh of deviltry and hellishness. In this sense he is the anti-Christ, the man of sin of whom the Bible speaks."[82]

A Respite from the Rhetoric

As they busied themselves with domestic concerns, Minnesota's housewives could find a respite from the war rhetoric and still do their part at home to support the war effort. With the potential for food shortages looming as the

Food conservation was a major homefront effort during the war years. *Courtesy of the Minnesota Historical Society.*

war intensified, local officials launched a major food conservation effort in early April. In announcing a Food for Victory conference to be held at the Minneapolis Auditorium, Luther Farrington, the conference chairman, reminded his male colleagues, "Women of Minneapolis so far have done most of the work and learned most of what needs to be known about the food problem. This [conference] is the first opportunity for men to inform themselves about the problem, as it is today."[83]

As a conservation measure, the U.S. Agriculture Department issued a directive calling on grocers to match sales of wheat flour to their customers with an equal amount of wheat substitutes, including barley flour, buckwheat and rolled oats. The Minneapolis-based Pillsbury Flour Mill Company told its customers, "Patriotism does not stop with *buying* these substitute cereals. If the object of the Food Administration is to be realized in the saving of wheat, the wheat substitutes must actually be *used*. Otherwise no savings of wheat is accomplished, and there is besides a waste of valuable foods that is very serious under present conditions."

Upper-income Minnesota women, who rarely spent time in the kitchen, could do their part to aid the war effort by volunteering with the Red Cross. If they lived in St. Paul, they could join that city's local chapter, formally organized on April 16, 1917, just ten days after the United States issued its war declaration. In his account of St. Paul's involvement in the war, Franklin Holbrook wrote about the local women who volunteered with the St. Paul chapter:

> *Nearly fifteen thousand workers, including an occasional male enthusiast, sewed, knitted and rolled bandages for the Red Cross. Society women who had been accustomed to having every service performed for them, faithfully labored*

The Red Cross provided an opportunity for women from all social classes to do their part on the homefront. *Courtesy of the Minnesota Historical Society.*

day after day at the sewing machines or at the long tables, and busy housewives who heretofore found every minute of their day occupied with the care of their own homes and families now somehow managed to find time to knit for those sons and brothers who were away from home comforts. Most remarkable of all, perhaps, were the services rendered by hundreds of girls, who after working all day in stores, offices and factories conscientiously appeared at the workshops in the evening to offer their services to the Red Cross.[84]

With the end of the war in November 1918, the work of the St. Paul chapter, along with other chapters throughout the state, would start winding down. But unlike other short-lived homefront efforts during World War I, the Red Cross would continue to have a major presence in Minnesota well into the twenty-first century.

THE POLITICS OF WAR

On April 4, 1918, the *Minneapolis Journal*'s front page was filled with news about the American troops, who were battling to hold back the German surge on the western front. Stuck away in its back pages, the *Journal* ran a small story about a former Minnesota congressman who had just filed as a candidate for governor. The paper reported that Charles A. Lindbergh of Little Falls had listed himself as a Republican although he was endorsed by an organization known as the Nonpartisan League.

As reported in the *Journal*, Lindbergh made no direct reference to the war in his filing statement. Rather, in dramatic terms, he declared that America's "vast resource…had fallen into the

Charles Lindbergh's son, pictured here with his father, would become one of the twentieth century's most iconic figures. *Courtesy of the Minnesota Historical Society.*

hands of monopolists we are forced to patronize. This has given the profiteers the privilege of levying a tribute on the workers." Then, sounding a theme that would be echoed nearly a century later by like-minded activists, Lindbergh went on to declare that "less than 2 percent of our population owns 65 percent of the wealth." The former congressman maintained that "this condition is wrong and injurious to the best interests of our country. Indeed, our country cannot survive unless this situation is corrected.[85]

The *Journal* story did not indicate whether the candidate's young son was with his father when the elder Lindbergh filed for office. In later years, the son would become one of the twentieth century's most iconic figures.

WINDS OF PROTEST

Charles Lindbergh's campaign quest was shaped by a political movement that had emerged only a few years earlier in Minnesota's neighboring state of North Dakota, launched by a wily entrepreneur named Arthur Townley. The war in Europe was not yet on the horizon when Townley found himself on the verge of bankruptcy. Once known as the Flax King of North Dakota, Townley watched his eight-thousand-acre kingdom collapse in 1912 when the price of flax dropped by two-thirds, pushing him $80,000 into debt.

The dethroned king believed that price fixing by Minneapolis grain merchants led to his downfall and he vowed to seek political retribution. A shrewd and self-taught student of politics, he surmised that both of the two major political parties were beholden to the state's corporate interests, so he set out to overturn the existing political order in his adopted state of North Dakota. For a while, Townley, a native Minnesotan, flirted with socialism but then turned away from the radical activist organization when he decided that its program was too broad. "They wanted to take over everything," he later said. Even so, he borrowed key planks from the socialist platform that he knew would appeal to the state's populist-minded farmers. For years, many of them had railed against the big-business interests—the railroads, bankers and grain dealers—they saw controlling their economic future. To appeal to North Dakota's farmers, Townley espoused a distinctively midwestern version of socialism that called for a state-owned bank, publicly owned grain elevators and state regulation of railroad rates.

Like the Tea Party leaders of the twenty-first century, Townley decided against forming a third political party. Instead, he devoted his energies to building the Nonpartisan League into a grass-roots pressure group. But Townley's organization was anything but nonpartisan. Its strategy was to

This page and next: In 1918, the Non-Partisan League supported Charles Lindbergh's bid to unseat incumbent Republican governor Joseph A.A. Burnquist. *Courtesy of the Minnesota Historical Society.*

endorse candidates in the Republican Party, elect them and then take control of the party machinery. In the 1916 election, Townley's grass-roots pressure group was wildly successful, sweeping into office virtually a full slate of NPL-backed candidates.

Word of Townley's success filtered over into Minnesota, and soon he was encouraged to work his political magic in his home state. His organizers spread out through the state's rural counties, signing up farmers who were hopeful that the Nonpartisan League could achieve the same political result for them that it had achieved next door in North Dakota.

In February 1917, the league moved its headquarters to St. Paul and convened grass-roots meetings to elect delegates to the NPL's legislative conventions. These local political assemblies, in turn, would elect delegates to a state convention. In March 1918, the league held its first statewide conclave in Minnesota. Following its North Dakota playbook, the newly organized Minnesota affiliate decided to run candidates in the June Republican primary. The NPL-endorsed candidates would seek to defeat the Republican organization's endorsees, including the incumbent Republican governor, Joseph Burnquist.

AN ARDENT PROGRESSIVE

To oppose Burnquist, the NPL selected Charles A. Lindbergh Sr. as its standard bearer. Lindbergh had served four terms in the U.S. House representing Minnesota's Sixth Congressional District but had given up his seat before the United States entered the war. A successful lawyer from Little Falls who also dabbled in real estate before he went to Washington, Lindbergh was the embodiment of small-town Scandinavian Lutheran rectitude. His somber demeanor and dark clothing gave him an air of respectability that was a political plus during his hard-fought battle with Burnquist.

But Lindbergh was not always what he appeared to be. Behind the black suit and the starched collar, he was an ardent progressive who had supported Teddy Roosevelt's Bull Moose insurgency in 1912. During his four terms in Congress, he had moved even farther left, speaking out frequently against the groups he called "the money trusts"—the secretive organizations that, he said, had an iron grip on the U.S. economy. The NPL's gubernatorial candidate had been firmly opposed to the U.S. entry into the war. Most likely, he would have voted against the April 1917 war declaration if he had still been in Congress when the resolution came before the House.

His 1917 book, *Why Your Country Is at War*, provided ample political fodder for his foes in Burnquist's camp. In the book, Lindbergh was careful to voice his support for the war effort once it was underway. Nonetheless, his commentary contained passages that would come back to haunt him during the campaign. Most notable was the phrase "We should spurn as contemptable to the idea of democracy the oft-heralded statement of 'Stand by the President.'" Lindbergh went on to declare that the statement was often used as a cover to deceive the public. But that context was conveniently ignored by Lindbergh's critics.[86]

According to Minnesota historian Carl Chrislock, "since standing by the president came to rank with God and country, the [Nonpartisan] League opposition got considerable mileage out of this apparent rejection of the highest duty of citizenship."[87]

In addition to his statements about the war, Lindbergh was also saddled by a resolution he had introduced in Congress that had offended the local Catholic bishops. The unfortunate wording of the resolution called for an "investigation" of the Catholic Church and the groups that were accusing it of improper political activities. Lindbergh intended the investigation to clear the air about charges and countercharges that were swirling around certain Catholic groups in his district, but church leaders took offense at the resolution. The bishop of St. Cloud even announced from the pulpit that he was praying for Lindbergh's defeat in the upcoming election. The controversy over the resolution clearly undercut the support Lindbergh might have expected to receive from the state's German Catholics, many of whom shared his misgiving about the war even while supporting efforts to win it.

Like its standard bearer, the Nonpartisan League had reconciled itself to the war by 1918 and issued statements, albeit guarded ones, in support of the war aims. But these did little to deflect the League's opponents, who were gaining political mileage with their charge that the NPL was disloyal. "Success or failure in the forthcoming campaign depended on meeting this challenge effectively," Chrislock noted. "To meet the challenge, the NPL paid proper deference at its 1918 convention to the flag, the Red Cross and the sacred obligation of all Americans to purchase liberty bonds. The platform proclaimed all-out support of the crusade against German autocracy, wholeheartedly endorsed President Wilson's war aims, and pledged continued support for all war activities."[88]

ON THE DEFENSIVE

Despite its public pronouncement about the war, the league found itself on the defensive throughout the campaign. On the surface, the campaign appeared to be all about loyalty and patriotism, but there were deeper issues driving a pivotal election that could determine that state's political and economic future.

Minnesota's corporate interests viewed the Nonpartisan League, and it's avowedly socialist platform, with alarm and were determined to halt its move into Minnesota. For them, a Lindbergh victory raised the specter of state ownership of banks and grain elevators and strict regulation of railroad and freight rates. The U.S. entrance into World War I gave these interests a convenient hammer they could use to beat the league into submission.

Inadvertently, the league might have handed the hammer to its opponents with its ill-advised gesture of inviting Governor Burnquist to address its 1918 convention. Burnquist angrily rejected the invitation, with a sharp blast at the left-leaning organization. In his rejection letter, he maintained that the league had been "closely connected with the lawless IWW and the Red Socialists." Moreover, the league had "catered to that faction of labor which has violated the law and been opposed to just orders of duly constituted authority." Then, continuing his attack, the governor declared that "the unpatriotic utterances...at your last convention put a stamp of disloyalty [on the league] that can never be erased."[89] Burnquist's letter provided an official stamp of approval by the state's highest elected official on the charges of disloyalty continually levied at Lindbergh and his political supporters.

The league's political liabilities were exacerbated by developments on Europe's eastern front when the newly installed Leninist regime in Russia signed a peace treaty with Germany in March. Many on the left in Minnesota had spoken favorably about the Russian revolution. Now, they were tarred as apologists for the evil "Bolshevikee," who were in league with America's sworn enemies, the "Huns."

For his part, Burnquist tried to stay above the political fray after his attack on the league. He announced that he would not engage in political debates and that he would limit himself to patriotic addresses while the war was still raging in Europe. This seemingly nonpartisan stance provided an opportunity for the Public Safety Commission, in effect, to become an arm of the Burnquist campaign by arranging for the governor to deliver his patriotic addresses all over the state during the months leading up to the June primary.

The commission's fiery John McGee made no secret of his political leanings with his intemperate remarks that caused a short-lived backlash for the Burnquist camp. In an April statement to a congressional committee in Washington, McGee thundered that a "Nonpartisan League lecturer is a traitor every time. In other words, no matter what he says or does, a League worker is a traitor. Where we made a mistake was in not establishing a firing squad in the first days of the war. We should now get busy and have that firing squad working overtime." But then, McGee made a major political gaffe when he declared that the disloyal element in Minnesota "is largely among the German-Swedish people. The nation blundered at the start of the war by not dealing severely with these vipers."[90]

Carl Chrislock later commented on the political fallout from this ill-advised statement. "To condemn German Americans as a group was one thing, but to take on the state's Swedish American community, as well, bordered on political madness."[91] Prodded by Burnquist's handlers, McGee later back tracked, claiming that he had been misquoted and that he had not intended to impugn the loyalty of Swedish Americans, but the damage had been done.

Still, Lindbergh remained on the defensive over the loyalty issue as he and his supporters campaigned throughout the state. In the months leading up to the June primary, NPL campaigners found that they were often barred from holding meetings in communities dominated by avid loyalists. In some cases, they were physically attacked by angry mobs. In May, NPL organizer Nels Hokstad was tarred and feathered as he attempted to address a league rally in Central Minnesota.

Lindbergh himself was vilified during the final weeks of the campaign. One Minnesota historian later recalled that "violence followed Lindbergh everywhere. His opponents spied on him continually; he was banned in Duluth and hanged in effigy in Red Wing. Several times, unruly mobs dragged him from the speakers' platform. On one occasion, Lindbergh came out of a meeting to find his driver badly beaten. He convinced the assembly mob to allow them to leave, only to be answered by a shower of bullets as the automobile drove away."[92]

On June 8, ten days before the Minnesota primary, Lindbergh was arrested in the town of Elm Creek by the Martin County sheriff on charges of violating the state's sedition law. The charges were later dismissed, but the NPL's gubernatorial candidate was forced to face the voters on June 17 with the charges still hanging over his head.

While Lindbergh did not succeed in his effort to oust Burnquist on election day, he came closer than many political observers had predicted, winning a respectable 43 percent of the vote. The 1918 primary sounded the death knell for the Nonpartisan League in Minnesota. Never would it be able to replicate its early victory in North Dakota. But a new political movement rose out of the NPL's ashes. In November 1918, a coalition of

NPLers and labor unionists ran under the "Farmer Labor" label for the first time. The coalition would later become a full-fledged political party in Minnesota and achieved great success when it elected the charismatic Floyd Olson as governor of Minnesota in 1930.[93]

CITY HALL RADICAL

Meanwhile, in Minneapolis another controversial figure was fighting for his political life during the 1918 midterm election campaign. Two years earlier, Thomas Van Lear had been elected mayor, much to the chagrin of the city's business leaders, who were horrified by Van Lear's outspoken political views. An avowed socialist and a powerful orator, the newly elected mayor had built a loyal following in the city's working-class wards during his earlier election campaigns, when he had come close to toppling the local Republican political establishment.

In 1914, while he was running for a congressional seat, Van Lear gave a fiery address to his supporters. He told the cheering crowd, "When fat, slick, well dressed men, who never missed a meal in their lives, come down here and tell you workingmen that you should be patient and satisfied with things as they are, I think you ought to tell them to go to hell!"[94]

Before entering politics, Van Lear had worked as a union organizer for the International Order of Machinists. As he moved up the union hierarchy, Van Lear used his organizing skills to energize the anemic local affiliate of the Socialist Party of America. Before 1910, the socialist organization in Minneapolis was "little more than a skeleton," according to labor historian David Paul Nord. "Van Lear and his followers put flesh on it," Nord noted.[95]

Nationally, the Socialist Party was gaining a loyal following and nearly one million votes for its presidential candidate, Eugene Debs, in the election of 1912. Locally, Socialists were achieving some electoral successes in widely scattered labor strongholds while Van Lear was organizing in Minneapolis. Their first big win came in Milwaukee, where a party loyalist, Emil Seidel, was elected mayor in 1910. Over the next four years, the Socialists would elect mayors in places like Butte, Montana; Berkeley, California; and Schenectady, New York.

In Minneapolis, Van Lear finally succeeded in winning the city's top political job in 1916 after coming close in two previous tries. Only days before the November 7 election, the *Minneapolis Tribune* raised the specter

Thomas Van Lear (above, left) was elected mayor of Minneapolis in 1916 with strong support from the city's labor movement. Many local business leaders were outraged that an avowed socialist was now occupying the mayor's seat in city hall (above, right). *Courtesy of the Hennepin County Public Library Special Collections.*

of a socialist takeover of city hall. The paper maintained that Van Lear's election would put the mayoralty "in the hands of a secret, irresponsible, possibly non-citizen inner circle."[96] On election day, the voters disregarded the *Tribune* warning and elected Van Lear, giving him 55 percent of the vote in his contest with the Republican-backed Hennepin County sheriff, Otto Langum.

In November 1916, international events had not yet cast a shadow on local politics in Minneapolis. Woodrow Wilson had just been reelected president on the slogan "He Kept Us Out of War." As an avowed socialist, Van Lear, like many left-leaning activists of his day, viewed American militarism in economic terms—as an effort by the corporate interests to tighten their hold on the U.S. economy.

WAR CLOUDS

On April 7, 1917, only a day after Congress declared war on Germany, Van Lear's Socialist Party of America met in emergency session in St. Louis. In what came to be known as the St. Louis Platform, the SPA adopted an incendiary resolution, branding the war "a crime against the people of the United States." The resolution called for "vigorous resistance" to the draft and to any efforts aimed at limiting labor union organizing.[97] Like Lindbergh, Van Lear became a reluctant supporter of the war while continuing to condemn those who sought to profit from it. But the newly elected mayor refused to disavow the St. Louis platform, a stance that his opponents would exploit in 1918.

Van Lear did not try to hide his Socialist connections, but as a shrewd politician, he tried to deflect attention away from those connections and toward his own local agenda. During one campaign event, he remarked that his opponents wanted him to give an "academic talk on socialism." But he told his audience that he had rejected that suggestion, saying, "I am so busy telling people how to avoid being robbed by the street railway company that I have no time to give an academic talk on any subject.[98]

In 1916, the local street railway firm, the Twin City Rapid Transit Company (TCRTC), had emerged as a major issue in Van Lear's mayoral campaign. That year, municipal officials were preparing to renegotiate the city's franchise agreement with the transit company, which had been scheduled to expire in 1923. Under the terms of a recently passed state law, the city and the company were able to negotiate a new agreement prior to 1923 if both parties chose to do so. Van Lear charged that a pending franchise plan was rigged in favor of the company. The right course of action, he maintained, was public ownership of the street car system. But if that could not be achieved, he wanted the current agreement to remain in place until its original expiration date seven years later.

Van Lear might have wanted to focus on local targets like the TCRTC once he took office on January 2, 1917, but he soon found that homefront preparedness was becoming a preoccupation in Minnesota after war was declared in April. That spring, local officials, including Hennepin sheriff Otto Langum, Van Lear's opponent in the previous year's election, were preoccupied with the upcoming military draft registration scheduled for June 6.

Fearing disruptions and demonstrations by draft opponents on registration day, Langum announced that he had assembled a large crew of special deputies to maintain order on June 6, but the mayor did not share the sheriff's concerns. Earlier in the month, Van Lear attempted to allay fears about possible disturbance when he told local reporters that he did not anticipate any problems when the city's young men appeared at the local registration centers to sign up for the draft. The draft was a complicated political issue for Van Lear. As mayor, he urged compliance with the registration laws even while his political party, nationally, had called on its followers to resist them.

Earlier in the week, a member of Van Lear's mayoral staff, Anna Maley, had become embroiled in an internal socialist party dispute over a leaflet circulated by some Hennepin County socialists who appeared to urge opposition to registration and the draft. Maley maintained that the statement did not represent an official position adopted by the local Socialist Party organization, but other party members disputed her view and attempted to censure her for what they considered her prowar stance.

Maley's title was "stenographer," but she was more than just another member of the city hall clerical staff. A nationally known Socialist activist in her own right, Maley was a member of the national party's executive committee and was considered one of the party's intellectual leaders. In Van Lear's office, she functioned as his political confidante and second in command. In a later time, she would have had the title of deputy mayor.

For Van Lear, the draft was more than a political issue. It was also a family matter. His son, Ralph, who shared his father's Socialist views, was draft age. The younger Van Lear had applied to his local draft board for an exemption, citing his membership in the Socialist Party and his antiwar political beliefs.

But his exemption was denied. He was later drafted and served as a private with the U.S. Army's 337th Field Artillery unit.

In November 1917, the *Tribune* reported that Ralph had recently been released from the guard house at Camp Dodge in Iowa after being imprisoned for "sanitary violations." The paper did not provide more details about the nature of the younger Van Lear's transgressions, but Ralph probably did not have an easy time in the army, given the widespread knowledge about his father's actions in Minneapolis and his own effort to seek a draft deferment.[99]

Even as he tended to the day-to-day business of the city, Mayor Thomas Van Lear continued to give speeches around the state espousing his firmly held Socialist views. In the town of Glencoe, Van Lear was reported to have declared in August 1917 that "the war was not a struggle for democracy but inspired by Wall Street and the munition workers, and the boys who fell in the conflict would be sacrificed, not for democracy but for commercialism."[100]

The speech enraged members of the Minnesota Bar Association, who drafted a resolution calling for Van Lear to be removed from office by the Public Safety Commission. The resolution was withdrawn just before the final vote when some Minneapolis attorneys noted that a stenographic transcription of the speech was not available, which meant that the bar association had no tangible evidence that it could present to the commission.

The next month, on September 29, Van Lear gave a widely reported speech to the Producers and Consumers Convention in St. Paul. The mayor told his sympathetic audience, "We have always found in the great shops, mills, and factories of this country that whenever the employer had the autocratic right to decree as he saw fit and all others must obey, that just at that moment we lost our liberty, at that moment we became industrial slaves."[101]

In its opinion page, the *Minneapolis Tribune* made clear its disdain for a mayor it believed was promoting dissent and even disloyalty while the country was at war. In an October 19 editorial entitled "Our 'War' Mayor," the paper declared, "We have, to be sure, a 'war' mayor, but the word 'war' in this connection does not signify the same thing as it does when the word is issued in conjunction with a governor or a president. In one case [referring to Van Lear], it is war against a frank avowal of loyalty to the city, the state and the nation."[102]

In December, Van Lear displeased the *Tribune* even more when he vetoed a Minneapolis ordinance that made city residents guilty of vagrancy if they made public statements considered seditious. In his veto message, Van Lear maintained that the ordinance could be used to suppress legitimate free speech. Moreover, he believed that the city already had sufficient laws on the books to deal with vagrancy. The city council voted to override the mayor's veto, but there is no evidence that the ordinance was enforced.

While he continued to speak about the war and its negative impact on American life, Van Lear was careful to voice his support for the war effort itself. In a speech to a neighborhood improvement group earlier in the year, Van Lear noted that "war has been declared and all of us must do our duty…but our duty lies in obeying the War Department orders, not those of the New York Chamber of Commerce, the Minneapolis Civic and Commerce Association or the newspapers. Don't let yourselves be stampeded, wait until the government tells you what it wants, and then do it. In that way, you will be good citizens."[103]

REELECTION BATTLE

When he launched his reelection campaign in May 1918, Van Lear addressed the issue of loyalty head on in a speech to 1,800 supporters at the Minneapolis Auditorium. He told the cheering crowd, "They [Van Lear's opponents] had to have some excuse to defeat the working class candidate, so they say this fellow Van Lear is not quite loyal. Every one of the candidates who have filed have inferred that [Van Lear] is not quite loyal by saying that he, himself, is super loyal and that the people need him above all else." Van Lear went on to condemn the Minneapolis aldermen who, in his words, "gave $420,000 out of your pocket into the pocket of the gas company. They would like to be elected again, not as friends of the gas company, but as patriots. Don't you see the trick? They could not be elected as friends of the gas company or as friends of the street railway company, but they hope to be elected as patriots and they hope to condemn some other men for lack of patriotism."[104]

Despite his efforts to deflect the loyalty issue, Van Lear found himself on the defensive as the mayoral campaign heated up in 1918. At a pre-primary candidate's forum at the end of May, the mayor was backed into a corner when the issue of the Socialist Party's St. Louis Platform was raised. When one of his primary opponents, W.F. Kunze, asked Van Lear if he supported the platform plank that called the U.S. war declaration "a crime," the mayor replied that it was not a city matter. But Kunze continued to press the issue. "Are the voters entitled to know where you stand on the St. Louis Platform?"

During his reelection campaign in 1918, Van Lear appeared on the same platform with the Non-Partisan League's Charles Lindbergh. The Van Lear–Lindbergh alliance was the start of a farmer-labor movement that would become a dominant political force in Minnesota in the 1930s. *Courtesy of the Hennepin County Public Library Special Collections.*

Kunze asked. "To this question, Mr. Van Lear replied 'Yes,'" the *Minneapolis Tribune* reported. "'Well, where do you stand,' the questioner asked. 'This isn't a local matter,' was the reply of Minneapolis's Socialist mayor."

The *Tribune*'s front page account of the forum clearly wounded Van Lear politically with a headline that read, "Mayor Van Lear Refuses to Repudiate Socialist Party's Anti-War Views."[105] Sensing he was in trouble, Van Lear was able to draw on support from the agriculturally based Nonpartisan League. The league's participation in Van Lear's campaign would help lay the foundation for an emerging farmer-labor coalition that would become a potent political force in Minnesota over the next twenty years.

After the June primary, Van Lear found himself facing J.E. Myers, a local businessman backed by the Republicans. As the campaign moved into its final days, Myers blasted away at Van Lear's socialist ties. "I know the moral fiber of the citizenship of Minneapolis. I know it has never failed to respond to the call of patriotism and I know the only real issue to be decided by the mayoralty election is the issue of Minneapolis and Americanism vs. Socialism," Myers declared.

"Men of Minneapolis," Myers continued, "this not a campaign between candidates. The issue has nothing to do with personalities. It is bigger than individuals. Next Tuesday, you will vote for or against Socialism. The political Socialism that laughs at our constitution as an anachronism, that seeks to destroy the ideals of modern civilization as represented by home and church, and substitutes for them, no one knows what. You will vote for or against Socialism that proposes to replace democracy with class autocracy—the Bolshevikism of Russia."[106]

On election day, Van Lear found that Myers had defeated him but just narrowly, by about 1,700 votes. The mayor attributed his defeat, at least in part, to the fact that so many of the city's young men were away from home in the service and unable to vote in the 1918 election. Van Lear said he "would continue to fight alongside the common people and against special privilege. We are not discouraged. If we are beat at this election, we will come back when the boys come back.[107] A week later, on November 11, the boys found that they could, in fact, start coming back. An armistice had taken effect. A year and half after the United States entered the Great War, it was finally over.

In many ways, Lindbergh and Van Lear were both political casualties of the war. But both men helped lay the groundwork for a new political movement that would have a long-lasting effect on Minnesota political life well into modern times.

6

CLIMACTIC BATTLES AT HOME AND ABROAD

The telegram from H.M. Bracken dated September 28, 1918, was brief and to the point: "Severe influenza Faribault County, Wells Village—100 cases reported following return of soldier from cantonment." The wire from Bracken, the head of the Minnesota Board of Health, to an unidentified federal official signaled that a worldwide epidemic had finally reached Minnesota.[108]

Considered the worst public health catastrophe since the bubonic plague of the thirteenth century, the influenza pandemic of 1918 moved swiftly throughout this country, killing 500,000 Americans, nearly ten times the number of battlefield deaths suffered by U.S. troops during World War I.

The pandemic had erupted as the war was reaching its climactic months in 1918. In an effort to maintain morale while the fighting was still underway, the three Allied powers—England, France and the United States—strictly censored reports of the outbreak of the illness among their troops. Because Spain was not a combatant, its news reports about the disease were not censored. As a result, the epidemic was linked to Spain and became known as the Spanish flu.

DISTURBING REPORTS

The virus-borne disease with no known cure was spread in this country by U.S. soldiers who contracted the illness in the training camps and brought the virus with them back to their home communities. The cantonment mentioned in H.M. Bracken's telegram referred to an army camp where the unidentified soldier had been stationed before he returned to Minnesota.

Gruesome reports soon began to circulate about the effects of the disease as it took hold of its victims' bodies. One commentator observed that "most did not die from the flu per se, but rather from a deadly form of pneumonia that often accompanied it. And many of those who died did so with extraordinary ferocity and speed, for this was no ordinary pneumonia. As their lungs become unable to transfer oxygen to the blood, they turned a strange color, a condition called cyanosis. Some victims turned so dark that rumors began to fly that the disease was not influenza, but the Black Death."[109]

An army camp physician wrote about the "purplish reddish greyish ashen color of the patient's face—chiefly around the lips but sometimes over the entire body. Hemorrhage was everywhere. Every sheet, towel, pillowcase, gown whether on a patient, doctor, nurse or orderly was purplish red. Many who died literally drowned in the bloody waters inside their own bodies."[110]

With U.S. soldiers living together in close quarters, the army camps quickly became huge incubators for the influenza virus. On October 1, army officials announced that twenty thousand new cases had been reported in the camps during the previous forty-eight hours. While many of the cases were relatively mild with good prognosis for recovery, an increasing number were progressing to life-threatening pneumonia. Fort Dix in New Jersey was particularly hard hit. There, sixty-one soldiers had died from the disease.

On October 1, the first influenza death occurred at Fort Snelling, where forty-two cases of the disease were confirmed. The University of Minnesota Hospital and the General Hospital in downtown Minneapolis were both reporting a surge in new cases. As the disturbing news began emanating from the area hospitals, local medical authorities began a concerted effort to educate members of the public about the steps they could take to avoid the flu—particularly if someone in their home was ill with the disease.

Dr. H.W. Hill, the executive secretary of the Minneapolis Public Health Association, cautioned that ill individuals should be kept in bed as long as their temperature persisted. "So far as possible, every patient should have a separate bed," Hill said. "One influenza patient may infect another with his particular complications and make the attack worse. Disinfect during the attack all discharges particularly from the nose and the mouth, handkerchiefs, bed linens and eating utensils."[111]

At Fort Dodge in Iowa, where many Minnesota soldiers were being trained, five hundred men had come down with the disease. The fort was under strict quarantine, with guards posted at the post entrances to keep out all visitors except those carrying a military pass. Post officials had wired an urgent request to the Red Cross for five thousand gauze masks used as a precautionary device for all patients and their attendants.

By the first week in October, civilian and military officials were estimating that the number of confirmed cases in Minneapolis had reached one thousand, with more than of half of those at Fort Snelling's military hospital. Dr. G.H. Guilford, the city's health commissioner, predicted that the epidemic had not yet crested here, with a marked increase in civilian cases expected over the next few weeks. Minneapolis General Hospital was under virtual quarantine, with two floors of the facility reserved for flu cases.

Guilford issued an urgent call for all new cases to be reported to the city health department so the spread of the disease could be tracked. The flu makes its appearance, he explained, when the patient experiences a sudden sensation of weakness, muscle aches and a high fever of from 101 to 105 degrees. The temperature subsides for a brief period and then reappears as the patient succumbs to pneumonia. If the influenza virus progressed that far, death was likely, Guilford said.

The city's health commissioner noted that the disease was extremely contagious and passed from person to person "at the speed of an express train" with the germs spread through discharges from the nose and throat.[112]

The surging epidemic put a huge strain on the state's medical personnel, particularly now that many health workers were away from home, serving in the military. The U.S. surgeon general began running ads in the local papers in an effort to recruit more nurses. One ad in the *Minneapolis Journal* entitled "The Nation Needs Nurses to Check Influenza" stated that "owing to the rapid spread of the present epidemic, the safety of this country demands that all patriotic nurses, nurses' aides, or anyone with experience in nursing place themselves at once at the disposal of the government."[113]

In the southern Minnesota town of Wabasso, the community's only physician, Dr. Frank Brey, worked virtually around the clock while the epidemic was at its peak. "It probably took five years off his life," noted one of his neighbors. Brey hired a driver who drove him from one town to another in a horse and buggy. The doctor slept while he was on the road, and the driver slept in a cot in the doctor's office while he was waiting to drive Brey on his rounds.

The Wabasso physician did what he could to ease the distress of his patients, even packing some of them in ice to bring down their fevers, but it often had little effect. "There was nothing, really, that anyone was able to do," noted the neighbor.[114]

CLOSING DOWN THE TOWN

As cases of the disease were reported with increasing frequency, communities throughout the state began taking steps to ban all public gatherings.

New Ulm's ban took effect on October 15. In his public announcement, J.H. Vogel, the town's public health officer, noted, "Within the last few days, a number of cases of Spanish Influenza have appeared in this city, and the disease appears to be spreading rapidly. It became apparent that unless measures were taken to present the spreading of the disease, we would have to look forward to quite an epidemic in this city." Vogel's notice, issued by New Ulm's Board of Health, went on to declare that, for the time being, "all schools, theatres and moving pictures houses, dance halls, bowling allies and other places where people congregated" were to be closed.[115]

The City of Minneapolis began taking steps to ban public gatherings on October 11. That same day, a new U.S. Army dispatch reported that flu deaths in the army camps were inching up toward eight thousand. In Minneapolis, the epidemic was on the upswing as reports of new cases poured into the city's health department. On October 10, the agency's head, Dr. G.H. Guilford announced that the city's 221 new cases represented a 50 percent increase over the previous day's report. At General Hospital, forty nurses had been stricken, forcing hospital officials to scramble to fill the vacancies created when so many of their own staff members were too ill to work.

The Minneapolis ban, ordered by the city council, took effect at 12:00 a.m. on Sunday morning, October 13. It applied to all churches, schools, theaters and dance halls. In his testimony to the council prior to its votes on the ban, Guilford said, "It [the flu] is not controllable by the usual means…It spreads in crowds and quarantine is of little value. The main thing is to keep people from getting close together."

"I don't want to scare the people, but it looks as though we will have a great many deaths from it in Minneapolis," Guilford added ominously.[116]

Across the river, St. Paul had not yet enacted its own ban by the end of the month. The *Pioneer Press* expressed anguished frustration about the lack

Opposite: As the flu epidemic took hold in Minnesota, the Minneapolis General Hospital was on the front lines of the battle to control the epidemic. General maintained a fleet of ambulances that kept hospital beds filled during the epidemic. *Courtesy of the Hennepin County Medical Center History Museum.*

of an effective response to the epidemic in its city. In a November 3 editorial entitled "In Heaven's Name Do Something!" the paper noted, "St. Paul enters a new week of the pneumonia surge with its confession of hopelessness repeated and nothing preventive or remedial in sight…From the medical side of authority comes the aggravating assurances that the conditions in St. Paul are better than in other cities and the disease is on the wane. It seems like a flimsy and incompetent apology for the inaction which is gradually arousing resentment in every quarter," the paper declared angrily.[117]

Prompted in part by the *Pioneer Press*'s strongly worded editorial, the St. Paul City Council did enact its own ban on public gatherings that following day, on November 4. But there was dissent about the council action from one influential source, Dr. H.M. Bracken, the head of the State Board of Health. Bracken, calling the Minneapolis ban "a joke," said he did not believe the closing order would do much to halt the spread of the disease. The state health official predicted that the epidemic would soon crest and then burn itself out.[118] By mid-November, that year's influenza wave in Minnesota did start subsiding, as Dr. Bracken had predicted that it would. There was a slight uptick in the incidence of the disease in early December but that wave soon dissipated as well. In 1918, 125,000 cases of the flu were reported in Minnesota, causing 7,260 deaths.[119]

SHRIEKING TRUMPETS AND SOLEMN REFLECTIONS

During the fall of 1918, the news from the homefront might have been disturbing, but the dispatches from the European front were triumphant. On October 12, while Minneapolis was ordering a ban on public gatherings, the *Minneapolis Journal* was telling its readers about the American troops' capture of the Argonne Forest battle zone in France. Calling it the "Greatest U.S. War Feat," the *Journal* quoted the *New York Times*'s Edwin James, who reported that the Argonne capture was "by far the biggest thing our troops have done. They have taken what was always regarded as an impregnable position; one for the possession of which hundreds of thousands of men have died in the last 50 months."[120]

By late fall, even as the influenza pandemic was peaking, the four-year-old war was finally winding down. On November 6, the Kaiser's government sent its representatives to meet with the Allies' military leader, Marshall Ferdinand Foch, to begin negotiations for a ceasefire. Foch ordered his

CLIMACTIC BATTLES AT HOME AND ABROAD

BURYING OLD INFLU ENZA

During the height of the flu epidemic, there were some light-hearted moments, according to this report from the November 7, 1918 *Minneapolis Journal*:

> *With a chorus of sneezes and sniffles as a requiem, Influ Enza,*
> *unlamented was buried with military honors by students*
> *at the army mechanics training camp at the University of*
> *Minnesota today. A stuffed figure, doing postmortem duty as*
> *the deceased, was given over to a group of pallbearers and*
> *then placed under the sod.*
> *While the last rites were being said, the mourners chanted*
> *to the tune of "John Brown's Body":*
>
> *We've got the Spanish Influenza*
> *We've got the Spanish influenza*
> *We've got the Spanish influenza*
> *That's why we can't get out.*

According to the *Journal*, "the mortuary travesty was indulged in because students at the training camp have been unable to obtain passes on account of the influenza epidemic."

troops to silence their guns to permit the Germans to pass through to French territory. A war correspondent from the United States mistook Foch's order for a sign that the armistice had been signed and wired his inaccurate report back to New York. Almost immediately, papers all over the country began trumpeting the news that the war was over. "Hip Hip Horray," Minnesota's *New Prague Times* declared joyfully on November 7, "Word came over the wires today that Germany had accepted the Allies armistice terms."[121] But this announcement was premature. The actual armistice would not be signed until five days later, on November 11.

When more accurate news reached Minnesota about the November 11 event, spontaneous celebrations sprang up all over the state. "Rochester was slow in realizing that the war was over," the city's *Daily Post and Record* reported, "but once it did, WOW! How it tooted things up today! When the sunrise came, it looked down on a city as tranquil as a midsummer afternoon in Sleepy Hollow. And then the first trumpet of the coming army of enthusiasts was heard. An automobile swung madly around the corner with horn honking incessantly. The driver of another car was attracted to the sound and soon came others, and soon what a din was there."[122]

"Winona simply went wild," the *Winona Daily Herald* reported on November 12. "Approximately 25,000 people had a hand in the joy-making. At 2:15 Monday morning, it began. At 2:15 Monday afternoon, it was increasing. At 2:15 this morning, the demonstration began to quiet down, but the spirit was still there.[123]

The news about the armistice reached the Twin Cities just before two in the morning. "A big siren tore the midnight silence, with a roar and a series of crescendo shrieks echoing from the hills of Columbia Heights to the lowlands of the Minnesota Valley," the *Minneapolis Journal* declared enthusiastically. "Soon Minneapolis sprung [*sic*] to life as lights flashed on all over town. Within minutes, people came pouring out of their homes and jumping on to the nearby trolley cars making their early morning runs," the *Journal* reported. "Milk trucks and milk wagons were pressed into service. Automobiles came out of their garages and every driver felt it his duty to come downtown, carrying as many wayfarers he could find to pick up."

"The constantly growing crowds outrivaled in noise making any other celebration in the history of the northwest. Horns, bells, loads of tin-ware dragged over the pavement at the tails of automobiles and trucks, drums, rattles, guns—everything blended into a mighty kinder symphony," the paper observed approvingly.

"By 4 a.m., the downtown streets were clogged with merrymakers. Everyone was brimming over with good humor and feeling of fellowship for every other man, be he struggling newsboy working his way through the crowd or the sedate banker off the hill blowing his horn till the veins on his neck were wreathed in purple expansion," the *Journal* reported.[124]

At the Leamington Hotel, two permanent residents, former Minnesota governor Samuel Van Sant and Judge Eli Torrance, woke up at 2:00 a.m. and joined the revelers. Both were Civil War veterans and past commanders of that war's veteran group, the Grand Army of the Republic. By 4:00 a.m., dressed in their GAR uniforms, the two men were marching around the block in a parade led by an Elks band. "We kept going until day light," Torrance later noted. "Pretty good for two old soldiers."

Later in the day, Minneapolis mayor Thomas Van Lear, issued a proclamation declaring November 11 a holiday and requesting all stores and businesses to close at 2:00 p.m. in observance of the armistice. "Our gallant boys in Europe have brought peace to a war torn world," Van Lear declared. "From the hearts of the mothers of this country, a load of anguish and anxiety has been lifted. Today, in spirit she stands with her boys on the battlefield and thanks the Creator for the blessing of peace."[125]

Near the front lines in France, the armistice was greeted with weary relief by Minnesotans serving in the U.S. Army's 151st Field Artillery. "There was no cheering nor excitement, though finally the conviction spread that the fighting had actually ceased," Louis Collins, a member of the Minnesota unit later remembered. "The fighting was ended, but the strain of the

Top: Colonel George Leach's *War Dairies* provided a firsthand account of his battlefield experiences. *Courtesy of the Hennepin County Public Library Special Collections.*

Right: Spontaneous celebrations occurred all over Minnesota when word reached here that the armistice had been signed. *Public domain.*

last few months had done its work. To those who had been toiling for weeks, the end of the war meant little for the time being, but warmth and sleep meant much."[126]

In his diary, Colonel George Leach, the 151st's commanding officer, noted the "absolute silence" in his army camp when the armistice was announced. Leach saved his outpouring of joy for his unit's triumphant return to Minnesota in May 1919:

> *Home! Daylight! The familiar fields, woods and streams of Minnesota. As we passed through the village, we were greeted with cheers from the people in the streets. Far off, whistles of the factories blowing. Soon South Saint Paul. We were nearing home. At last, the station, the old station of Minnesota's capital.*
>
> *A sea of wives, mothers, sisters, fathers, some of them wearing the uniform of the Union Army. I feared for the very life and limb of the men, as those loved ones with tears and laughter waited them. The streets were lined solid with humanity…It was a solemn moment, for the boys who marched and spectators who watched.*[127]

Epilogue

JUNE 12, 1921

Theodore Wirth was proud of his trees.

As the head of the Minneapolis Park System, Wirth had made a nationwide search to find just the right species of American elm for his latest project. He finally found what he wanted in Illinois and Virginia, where nurseries in both states could provide the trees that met his specifications.

Wirth would later write: "I was most anxious that the elms should be of a selected type as to uniformity and habit of growth so that in their ultimate maturity the magnificence of their stately beauty, symmetrical type, and majestic growth would be gloriously manifest."[128]

Wirth's prized elms were to be used for a unique tribute to the men and women from Minnesota's Hennepin County who had lost their lives during World War I. Unlike most war memorials consisting of a single monument, this commemorative installation was three miles long. Known as Victory Memorial Drive, it was a tree-lined parkway, running through the city's northwest corner. The idea for the memorial had taken shape in 1919 when members of Minnesota's 151st Field Artillery made a triumphant return to their home state after spending much of the previous year on the front lines in France.

As plans moved ahead for the Memorial Drive, the elms, still only saplings, were planted in the Park Board nursery in 1919. Two years later, by the summer of 1921, the saplings, now "magnificent specimens, "according to Wirth, were transplanted to the parkway. In front of each one, a marker listed the name of a fallen Minnesotan.

The Memorial Parkway's dedication ceremony on June 12, 1921, attracted thirty thousand visitors, who stood by as a formation of army airplanes flew overhead, sprinkling flowers down on to the parkway. In a message to the visitors and the assembled dignitaries, Charles E. Loring, the park board's former president, said "The trees we plant today will, on each recurring Spring, put on their beautiful robes of green to remind our children and their children's children for many generations to come, of the great debt we owe to the heroes whose memories they will ever keep green."[129]

In his address, Louis Collins, then Minnesota's lieutenant governor and a former member of the 151st Field Artillery, echoed Loring's words. "Nothing could be more appropriate as a memorial to our dead than this beautiful driveway," Collins declared. "In these trees we have a combination of sentiment and utility. Loving hands will care for these living memorials to the dead, the hands of Minnesotans for generations to come. Children will visit this driveway and in these and in the sentiments connected with them find typified the spirit of America."[130]

Over the years many of Theodore Wirth's prized elms have been replaced. But well into the twenty-first century, Victory Memorial remains this state's most enduring reminder of the sacrifices made by so many Minnesotans to end the first great war of the twentieth century. Tragically enough, that bloody conflict, which claimed the lives of 2,227 Minnesotans, never lived up to its promise. It would never become "the war to end all wars," as so many had hoped.

Opposite: Well into the twenty-first century, Minneapolis's Victory Memorial has remained one of the most enduring reminders of the sacrifices made by Minnesotans during America's first "Great War" of the twentieth century. *Author's collection*.

Appendix I

BATTLEFIELD VOICES

History of Base Hospital 26

In the summer of 1918, as the war was entering its climactic stage, the American Expeditionary Forces (AEF) established a hospital center near the French village of Allery. The center was made up of ten self-contained medical units. One of the ten was organized by personnel from the University of Minnesota. Known as Base Hospital 26, the medical unit was led by Major Albert A. Law, a professor of surgery at the university's Medical School. The Minnesota-based hospital was staffed by 36 officers and 207 enlisted men. Later, they were joined by a contingent of 100 army nurses. The hospital continued to treat sick and wounded American soldiers until it was decommissioned in May 1919.

The breezy and often humorous recollections of the Minnesota hospital staff were compiled in a book entitled *History of Base Hospital 26*. No individual authors are listed for this firsthand account of life in a World War I army hospital. The preface states that the book "was published in its entirety by the members of Base Hospital 26—officers, nurses and men. The material has been collected and shaped by the unit as a whole, and the responsibility for the success of this volume to present in an honest way, our part of in the world's greatest struggle falls upon the shoulders of all of us."

Excerpts from the Base Hospital history are reprinted here.

Appendix I

The Senior Medics' Stories

This is the story of the thirteen senior medics who were born into an anomalous position, lived an anomalous life and achieved an uncertain distinction in their chosen field. It all began a long time ago when the war was only a month old. The senior class of the Medical School of the University of Minnesota wended their way to the lecture room on the second floor of Millard Hall to listen to a lecture in surgery from Dr. A.A. Law, all unsuspecting of what was in store for them. They were greeted, not by Dr. Law of the tortoise-rimmed glasses and silk underwear, but by Major Law, M.C., resplendent in a new uniform and filled with the dignity of a new and awful responsibility thrust upon him.

He told us how he was about to leave us to work among "those poor broken men in France." He told us once more of his Filipino expedition and how "his boys had followed him thru hell, God bless them!" A positive wave of patriotism following in the train of his melting eloquence.

And then he asked whether any of us would go with him to the shell-shattered fields of heroic France. Would we! Almost to a man we would esteem it a heaven-sent privilege to be the merest camp followers in his command. Twenty names were then and there added to the gilded ranks of Base Hospital 26.

Followed a period of waiting. It scarcely seemed long, so filled was it with the dreams of what we were going to do when we reached the scene of action. Daily we talked the situation over among ourselves and with our officers, who still continued teaching in the Medical School while they awaited their call. What glorious pictures of medical work without limit were spread before us by our enthusiastic instructors. We were a happy crowd!

All thru the summer we waited, daily expecting our call. School opened again. And, since there seemed no chance of an early departure, the enlisted medics entered their last school year as tho [sic] nothing unusual were to happen. Impatience and an expectant attitude are a poor ingredient to a life of serious study; it is doubtful whether we learned what was expected of us.

But deceptive fate, which made all things rosy when rosiness was necessary to our presence in the unit, stayed with us; definite orders taking us to Fort McPherson for training came before the semester finals exposed us.

With the orders there came a sudden uncertainty in the minds of some of the medics. For nine men followed their mysterious hunch and left our ranks. Into the breach thus made, stepped two more medics, making thirteen senior medics enrolled and ready to stay to the end.

112

Appendix I

Hospital Trains

The first hospital train received in Allery pulled into the center about 3:00 p.m., July 23, 1918, one month after the arrival of this unit in France. At that time Base Hospital No. 26 was the only hospital capable of receiving patients, and the facilities on hand where entirely inadequate to give the patients the proper attention that they justly deserved.

When the notice was received that a hospital train was due, everything was excitement, and the coming of a circus to a small town could in no way create more eagerness than that with which this train was looked forward to.

When the train finally pulled into the center, every member of the hospital was down alongside the tracks, anxious to obtain the first glimpse of a hospital train and the patients, which were at the time a great curiosity.

The enlisted men were lined up along the train and a detail of ten men were assigned to work inside the train, assisting the patients on the litters and passing them out of the car to the men who were assigned to carry them from the train to the Receiving Ward.

After the arrival of the first few hospital trains, patients ceased to be a curiosity, and the train detail soon resolved itself into a trying and difficult assignment. In order to systematize the unloading of the trains, a permanent detail of men was assigned to work inside the cars and another detail to assist in the handling of the patients from the train to the ambulance or litter team.

The patients on the trains were classified into two groups: the patients who were only slightly wounded or gassed being classified as walking cases, and the badly wounded classified as litter cases. The trucks employed for this were used in transporting walking cases and the ambulances for all litter cases.

In passing, a word should be said for the wonderful patience displayed by the men when being transferred from the trains. At best, it is very difficult to remove the patients without a great deal of pain to the patient, but the men displayed wonderful courage no matter how severe the injury and aided in every possible way their removal from the trains.

The Trip to Bordeaux

Base Hospital No. 26 boasted of what is known as a motor detail. It consists of a sergeant in charge, a mechanic in charge and drivers.

Motor transportation at the time was handled by each organization separately. After we became part of the AEF, we found that all transportation was pooled, and handled by a motor transport corps.

BH 26 being pioneers at Allery gave us the chance to furnish men for all the walks of army life. Motor trucks were needed immediately to carry on the work of construction. We had our opportunity offered then and there. Requisitions were put thru for five Packard trucks, three to be delivered to the hospital center at Beaune and two for Allery.

On the night of July 11 the detail was under pack and ready to hit for Bordeaux via the All-American train to Tours and the frog line to Bordeaux. We reached Tours about ten o'clock on the 12ᵗʰ and were guided by the always loving and tender MPs to an eat shop. A few "cofs," "café," "pomdetares," a bit of "Vin Blanc" and a sleepless night was forgotten.

About noon we got on the frog train. Our destination was reached at one o'clock the next morning, a fine time to hit a strange town in France. We awoke not less [sic] than ten hotel keepers only to get the answer "Complet," which signified that the place was full and we must keep going. The result was that we unrolled our blankets and "cooshayed" on the concrete bed upon which the depot did the same.

Morning came all too soon. It is hard to believe that concrete makes a good bed, but it is so nevertheless. After a good breakfast, our leader, Sir Edward, made his way out of the transportation park to get the lay of the land. The rest of us busied ourselves in giving Bordeaux the double O. Some town, is all that is needed in explanation.

Late in the afternoon, we finished Bordeaux and went to the Motor Park to be ready for work the next day. At 4:00 p.m., the sixteenth of July, "Old Shell Shock" gave the famous command "Crank Motors." With a mighty roar of throbbing engines, the motor detail of the "fighting 26" had started their career for better or worse. We covered about four hundred and twenty-five kilometers in six days, taking in a few good towns en route.

Most of our route carried us thru beautiful mountainous country. Many times we went steadily upgrade to reach the summit of the mountain. The road would run along for a few kilometers, then descend again into the valley. Off, first on one side then on the other would be the valley with its little villages of red tile roofs. Here and there a lovely château nestled amongst the trees on a hillside. The hillside grape vineyards of one color, the foliage of another, the small gardens and patches of ripened grain of still other hues, gave a blending of beauty indescribable.

When we pulled into Nevers the load of supplies were [*sic*] left at the motor park, and after a bite to eat started on. It was near 10 o'clock when we found a good place to camp out. We were a short distance from a farmhouse and had hardly stopped before the clatter of wooden shoes were heard upon the road. Two little girls and a boy came up from the farmhouse for a visit with Americans. We had a stock of stick candy along, so we treated. They had never seen such a thing before and wanted to keep it to look at instead of eating it. We compromised by giving them enough to do both. The mother and father came up soon after to get acquainted.

Woodworth got out his mandolin and Getch the mouth organ and they went at it. Never had such strange music floated over the fields of France. The audience was awed, and for nearly an hour listened to tunes they had never heard before and will probably never hear again. After the concert we were invited up to the farmhouse for a nip of vin rouge before retiring.

The next day being Sunday we planned to keep sleeping until eight o'clock. We found our plans ruined when six o'clock came and the three little kids woke us all up to say "bon jour." We got up, went to the family pump for our morning wash and were then in a good mood for breakfast. Ten of us ate 45 eggs in omelets and a great quantity of coffee.

After visiting awhile, we bade our good friends "au revoir" and once again with a roar, we were on our way. We reached Beaue the following morning, left three trucks and after a good breakfast proceeded to Allery. We reached there before noon and were glad of it. Although we were pure white with dust and somewhat weary of body, we were all happy and pronounced the trip a huge success.

THE BATHHOUSE

Cleanliness being next to Godliness made this institution a prime factor in the operation of our now famous institution.

When a man has been in the trenches night and day for from twenty-four to ninety-six hours and longer, it is a nine to one bet that he can use a bath. We gave him one whether his week was up or not and we didn't wait for Saturday night to do it either.

The patients were brought to the bathhouse after leaving the receiving wards. The litter cases were lined up to wait for a table…While they were waiting they were undressed and examined for "pets." In cases where pets were found, steps were taken to rid the men of same undesirables...The men were put on the bathing table and given a good hot bath, shampoo included, clean pajamas and back on the litter and off for his ward.

The job of getting the wounded men on and off the table with as little pain as possible was one that required careful handling. The patients were game and helped as much as they could in moving on and off the litters. They were all glad to get a good bath before being put to bed. Walking patients went thru the same routine except that they used showers in place of the tables.

OPERATING ROOM

Following certain well known activities at Belleau Woods and Chateau Thierry, where the American soldiers started something which must be continued without giving the enemy an opportunity to come back, it became evident that corresponding activity in all branches of the AEF must be necessarily increased, none more so than that of the Medical Dept. both on the lines and farther back.

Placed in a new camp, uncompleted on our arrival, and still under construction, it was advisable to get together necessary equipment as would enable us to care for the wounded soldiers who would arrive within a few days, despite the fact as yet no Medical Supply Depot or QM existed within the camp...A hurried trip to Is-sur-Tille with a requisition and two trucks produced some very necessary supplies with which to carry on. Meanwhile some of them scouted around the neighborhood towns purchasing surgical items which could not have been obtained otherwise and which were indispensable to the operating room.

The arrival of the first few trains will not soon be forgotten. Actually our first connection with the field of battle. Eager as we were to be in it ourselves, here was a first grim realization of what we actually wished to be in, like seeing a play from behind the scenes. And we did envy these maimed and mangled as we lifted them from the train to the receiving ward.

Following the arrival of the first train our work had started in earnest. Due to the congestion on the front and stress of circumstances, many soldiers were brought to the operating room with only the first aid dressing applied.

From the battlefield, excited with their success over the enemy, nervous and high-strung, following days and nights of severest test, it was not surprising that under anesthesia, they were anything but mild and docile. Two and three men were necessary to hold a patient on the table while a whole regiment could not keep them from talking.

If nurses were brought up in a home atmosphere, nurtured by undefiled English, they must have been rudely awakened as they listened to the voluble and explosive language and slang which was bellowed forth as the patient went under the ether. Quite frequently we were treated to a charge over the top by officers and sergeants as they led their men and lived over again the very scene for their being in the hospital.

There were many times when one train load of patients had just finished when another train would be reported due in an hour. At night the men would not go back to bed but would stretch out on the tables for much needed rest. Standing and working over these patients for four or five hours was not a restful task.

FURLOUGHS

When we arrived in Allery there was much work to be done, and all thru the summer it continued. But after we were really settled and the machinery was in good working order, one by one the men found some excuse to ask for a pass to Paris, Lyon or some other place of equal interest. Then came the regular four-day passes, given to every man in the outfit and spent principally in Paris, Lyon or Marseilles.

The men left Allery on the various leaves with their pockets full of francs, their hearts full of expectations and their bodies full of energy. They returned with empty pockets and fatigued bodies. Travel was exceedingly difficult for train connections were poor, and owing to increased traffic, they often had to stand up for hours at a time in a crowded coach.

Altho [sic] travel was miserable and the men often came back to camp broke and tired, it was these few furloughs as much as anything that kept the spirits of the men up and gave them something more definite than the end of the war to look forward to.

FINAL THOUGHTS

Ten years from now when you're telling your kid
Of the Allery Battle and all that you did,
And he asks of the trench or the enemy's horde,
Just tell him straight off that you worked in a ward
There isn't a doughboy or even a gob
That worked as you on the wardmaster's job
A war-cross, my boy, you never could win,
Because of the branch of the service you're in;
But your duty you did minus cheers and HURRAH
And you'd have gone to the front had it not been for Law.

Appendix II

THE 151ST FIELD ARTILLERY

The origins of the 151st Field Artillery extend back to the late nineteenth century, when it was established as a unit of the Minnesota National Guard. Then known as the 1st Field Artillery, it would later see action during the U.S. Army incursion into Mexico in 1916. In 1917, when this country entered the First World War, the Minnesota 1st, with 38 officers and 1,258 enlisted men, was federalized and became known as the 151st Field Artillery, a unit of the army's much-heralded Rainbow Division.

The exploits of the 151st were recorded by Louis Collins, a member of the unit, who was a reporter for the *Minneapolis Journal* before the war. Collins later served as lieutenant governor of Minnesota from 1921 to 1925. His *History of the 151st Field Artillery, Rainbow Division* includes entries from a diary kept by Colonel George Leach, the unit's commanding officer.

Collins's book, published by the Minnesota War Records Commission in 1924, remains the most complete account of Minnesotans' participation in the First World War. Edited excerpts from Collins's book are reprinted here, with entries from Leach's diary shown in italics.

MOVING OUT

On August 14, 1917, the First Minnesota Field Artillery received word that it had been assigned to the Rainbow Division. The news was received with the greatest enthusiasm by the regiment encamped at Fort Snelling. The announcement increased the men's energy and enthusiasm as they went about their daily tasks. From now on, the regiment was on its toes. But men were becoming more and more impatient to be off, and the tension increased as the days past. Finally, the long-awaited orders were received. The First Battalion left Fort Snelling on September 4 in two trains of twenty-five cars each, some freight cars and others tourist sleepers.

The men were in high spirits. Along the sides of the cars they had hung banners bearing slogans expressing the lack of regard in which they held the enemy. There were to be weeks of railroad and ocean travel, a long period of training, nine months on the firing line and five months of peaceful occupation of defeated Germany before the regiment would head for home again, but the men on board the two-section train were not worried about the future. They were going across!

A Difficult Passage

On October 18, the 151st Field Artillery, together with other units of the Rainbow Division, embarked for France. The transport of the American troops to Europe will always be regarded as one of the epic phases of the great struggle. During the early months, before the machinery of transport was in the smoothest running order, the transatlantic voyage was likely to be marked by many trials and tribulations. No more vivid account of such a voyage has appeared than that contained in the diary of Colonel Leach from which the following passages have been taken:

> *Friday, October 19: We are out of sight of land this morning, and there are several battleships and transports in sight. The ocean is calm. Morning spent in drill and exercise of men. With 6,000 men on board, each man is allowed 45 minutes twice a day on deck. I am in command of men in the aft part of the ship, including 600 Negro stevedores. The air below deck is getting very bad, and men are sick; the holds are tough places to live. Not enough deck room for all men at once. The sea is getting up. Life belts are worn all the time, and the ship is dark at night.*

> *Saturday, October 20: Four hundred miles east of Hatteras at sunrise. Sea is rough and most of the men are sick. The whole day is spent in*

drills and inspections below deck. So many officers are sick that it makes a tough day for the rest. The hold and the deck look simply hopeless with filth. Details for work get sick before they can report, and it is a constant fight to get things done.

Sunday, October 21: The sea is calm and the sky is blue. An inspection of the ship found that conditions have improved a little with not so many men sick…Measles and mumps broke out among my Negro soldiers today, and Companies F and G are quarantined below deck. This complicates an already tough situation…I am seasick and going on my nerve. I now have 4,000 men in my part of the ship with only one field officer to help.

Tuesday, October 23: Conditions are much improved. There are no new cases of measles in the hold…Only one man from the 151st is in sick bay. The general called me into his stateroom this evening and complimented me on the discipline and condition of my part of the ship, and also for staying on the job when I was sick.

Saturday, October 27: We worked all day making final arrangements for abandoning the ship in case of a disaster. We are four days off our destination. The air is like winter, and the water is very cold so that a plunge does not look as attractive as it did back in the Gulf Stream. From now on, we will be in the acute and submarine and mine danger zone.

Tuesday, October 30: This is our most dangerous day. We passed an abandoned lifeboat in the afternoon. We received a wireless that two German subs had been seen heading in our direction. The situation has been very tense all day. At 3:30 AM, a merchant ship was torpedoed ten miles ahead of us.

Wednesday, October 31: This morning in the rain we steamed up the Loire River and I had my first glimpse of France. It looked beautiful. At 6:30 PM, we tied up in the river at Saint Nazaire and spent the evening on board. Everyone feels very happy and relieved. This ends 14 days at sea under the most trying circumstances, but it has been the greatest experience of my life to date.

Appendix II

The German Prisoners

On November 11, the 2nd Battalion of the 151st left for Coetquidan, having been designated an advance party to prepare the new camp for the rest of the brigade. It proceeded by rail to Guer, a little town near Coetquidan, and from there, marched a distance of about eight kilometers, or five miles, to the new camp, located on the top of a hill commanding a good view of the surrounding country.

Many new sights and experiences awaited the Minnesotans at Coetquidan. There they first came in contact with German war prisoners; six thousand of them were in the camp, employed on the roads and artillery ranges. For the most part, they impressed the newcomers as a stolid, uninterested lot, dressed in their old gray uniforms with the initials "P.G."—*prisonnier de guerre*—on the backs of their coats and wearing their little round fatigue caps.

They were very dirty and very hungry. Held by the French to small, unvarying rations, they fought for choice morsels of bone and meat in the Americans' garbage piles. The American soldiers could not fail to sympathize with these prisoners, even though they were enemies. Despite orders to the contrary, many American solders slipped cigarettes and bits of food to the Germans when the officers were absent from the scene.

Christmas Over There

Christmas Day was like a rift in the clouds. The regiment staged a vaudeville and minstrel show with Lieutenant Charles Bradley as manager and Wilbur Smith and Scotty Burns as stars…A special dinner was served and packages were distributed, each of which contained toilet articles, socks and chocolate. Only a few men had received gifts sent to them personally by their families, and these impersonal bundles helped immensely.

The gifts were purchased with the proceeds of a benefit vaudeville performance planned by the *Minneapolis Journal* and staged in the Minneapolis Auditorium on March 7. They were sent to the officers and men of the 151st Field Artillery as a remembrance from the people of Minneapolis and St. Paul. In spite of transportation difficulties, the gifts arrived in time to be distributed before Christmas.

The following extract from a letter of thanks, written by one of the men, is worth quoting: "This is one of the best things the folks at home ever did. The gifts arrived at a time when the men were thinking of the ones [at] home and of the distance that separated them…Many of the boys were away from home at Christmas for the first time in their lives. It was a solemn, almost religious ceremony, that opening of the presents. We will never forget that we were not forgotten."

On to the Front Lines

The route to Lorraine lay south of Paris—through Versailles, Fontainebleau, Troyes and Chaumont. The unfamiliarity of the countryside and the certainty that their outfit was at last "going in" combined to make this first journey to the front more of a lark to the men than those that followed. Not a man was downhearted—at least no one would admit it. In each of the cars much of the talk dealt with the imminence of death, but its general tone was hardly characteristic of the usual discussion of this serious subject. "I'll give you a just a week to live" and "a month from now you will be thirty days dead" were the remarks typical of the outward attitude, at least, of the regiment.

The men were going in to do what they had come to do, and they were going in much as they would have gone to a musical comedy back in their home towns.

On February 20 and 21, the various units detrained in the vicinity of Baccarat, a little city famous for its cut-glass industry. The units began marching in the rain toward their positions in the line. As they marched along, they came upon evidence of the German offensive of 1914, and the physical discomfort was forgotten in the realization that, at least, they were on the scene of the actual fighting.

The Mud of Lorraine

For over a week, the 151st Field Artillery, new at the business of war, worked day and night, in rain and snow, building new gun positions and dugouts, erecting new barracks and hauling ammunition to the guns and supplies to the echelons and battery positions.

Never will the men forget the mud of Lorraine. Comrades may be forgotten, details of the fighting fade away and the marches and campaigns become hazy, but that awful February–March battle with the mud of Lorraine will stand out in their memories until the final taps are sounded over the last surviving member of the division.

For ten days, the men of the 151st ate in mud, worked in mud, slept in mud and dreamed of mud—when the mud would let them sleep. Every day, it rained or snowed, and the already villainous character of the mud became even more villainous.

Mud is mud, but there is no mud like the mud of Lorraine. It is the wettest in the world and the dirtiest; the most treacherous and the coldest; the deepest and by far the muddiest. Certain mud is praised for its curative powers and some people bathe in it by choice; the very young have even been known to eat it. But even the worms, not generally credited with any great amount of self-respect, have too much pride to live in the mud of Lorraine.

THE FIRST TEST

The first real test came on the night of March 3. Shortly after midnight the Germans began shelling an area in front of Badonviller, about equidistant from that town and Neuviller. The fire increased in intensity and at dawn the enemy laid down a barrage at the position occupied by the Third Iowa Infantry…The infantrymen who were attacked resisted valiantly, and they were supported by the artillery in the rear, with all batteries of the 151st coming into action. The Germans did not succeed in penetrating the Allied line and after considerable losses on both sides, their attack was repulsed.

On March 5, the 151st suffered its first casualties in battle. At noon on that day, while the men were in the mess line, the enemy, whose airplanes had been active over the lines during the two previous days, began shelling the positions occupied by the 1st Battalion. The guns of Battery C had been placed near the crest of a large, deep stone quarry, and dugouts in this quarry sheltered the men of the battery when they were not at the guns. Sargent Theodore Peterson of the Medical Corps; Lieutenant Alexander W. Terrell; and Privates Charles Danielson, Emil F. Kraft and Water C. Smith were severely wounded.

Peterson, after being hit, instructed the men of the Medical Corps to attend to other wounded men and directed them in their work. While the work of caring for the wounded was in progress, Peterson, tested for gas, refusing to permit his men to remove their masks.

Sergeant Peterson died that night in the hospital at Baccarat—the first man of the regiment to be killed in battle. For his heroism, he was posthumously awarded the Distinguished Service Cross and the French Croix de Guerre.

FIVE DAYS IN THE TRENCHES

The severe shelling begun by the Germans on March 15 continued for several days, during which every battery of the 151st was under heavy fire. The position of Battery C was shelled so effectively that, within a radius of one hundred yards, the ground looked as if it had been ploughed. The dugouts saved the men, but after [they had spent] five days in them, living entirely on cold rations while shells were falling above and around. Occasionally a direct hit knocked the men from chairs or bunks. Finally, the order to leave the sector was issued, and it was thankfully received.

During these five days, most of the men at the gun positions had been unable to obtain water, and they had not been able to wash or shave. The "KPs"—men detailed daily to work with the cooks—were perhaps the only ones in gun positions who found any joy at all in the general condition. On the few occasions during these five days when fires were built in the kitchens in the positions among the trees, the KPs found that the German shells had already split their wood and they were saved the labor of cutting wood.

Ammunition came up every night, as drivers guided their teams along roads that were often the targets of German fire. When these trains of caissons arrived at the battery positions, the men were called out of their dugouts in the dark, and the work of carrying shells to the gun positions began…Occasionally, the work would be interrupted by enemy shell fire. The men at the gun positions did not envy the drivers, who had to work their way along dangerous roads at night. Telephonic communications between the batteries and the command posts were maintained with great difficulty. Telephone details were busy at all times of the day and night repairing lines broken by shell fire.

SPRING DAYS

May brought wonderful spring days to cheer the spirits of the men, who were still laboring at the guns and in the echelons; but with the good weather came greater aerial activity and the need for more camouflage. This meant more work. Green was becoming the predominant color, and every morning before daylight, the men were routed out to dig sod and cut boughs for camouflage purposes before the German aviators came over the lines.

It was during these days in Lorraine when, if it wasn't digging trenches or gun positions, it was digging sod. During these days, the artillery sang its refrain "As the caissons go rolling along," but it was sung with some lack of enthusiasm. The really popular ditty conveyed this sentiment:

They show you the horse that you are going to ride,
But they don't show you the shovel on the other side.

PREPARING FOR THE FINAL TEST

It was the good fortune of the 151st Field Artillery to help strike the blows that were to send the Germans reeling back to defeat. The regiment that arrived at LaChaussee-sur-Marne on June 23 was a very different organization from that which had gone into the Baccarat sector in February. True, its composition was the same, but it was a vastly superior fighting machine. Service in the front lines had smoothed the rough pieces and adjusted the loose parts. Four months in Lorraine had given the 151st a vigorous training in position warfare.

There, the men had learned how to build, occupy and conceal gun positions and dugouts. They had wallowed in the mud, soaked in the rain and lived on emergency rations. In Lorraine, they had first experienced shell fire, and there the first blood of the regiment had been spilled in combat. All this played its part in strengthening the regiment for the trials to come.

Rumors were rife during these days, and there was a general conviction that momentous events were impending. The regiment remained in the vicinity of LaChaussee-sur-Marne for less than a week and, then, on the night of June 28, moved to Courtisols, a town about eight kilometers east of Chalons-sur-Marne. The men's spirits were now keyed up to a high pitch. Rumors of a combined French-American offensive to be launched on July 4 spread among the soldiers billeted in Courtisols and the little towns back of the line. The idea of celebrating the Fourth with the usual noise, but with the Boche as the target, appealed to them, and they apparently took little account of the fact that such a procedure might be resented by German gunners.

Appendix II

The Alkali Desert

Day was breaking on the morning of July 5 as the batteries of the 151st rolled up to their positions north of Suippes. Here the men found themselves in an ugly, rolling chalk ridged country quite unlike the beautiful green Lorraine they had left behind. All was brown and barren, except in places where fir trees, thinned by shell fire, hinted of shade.

Along that sector of the front covered by the guns of the 151st Field Artillery, the French and German line were on the crest of considerable ridge that had at one time been wooded but that now, after three years of fighting, resembled a narrow strip from an alkali desert. This ridge, white and bald, was crisscrossed with trenches and barbed wire. On the French side of the hill, toward Suippes, the ground sloped gently down to a valley where the village of Souain had once stood. The hillside, at one time fertile ground, had been so systematically swept by fire and entrenched for fighting that almost no vegetation remained. The few trees left standing were crippled, and the very ground seemed blighted and burned.

The Strain of Waiting

The Allies awaited the onslaught of the enemy, improving positions and arranging the thousand and one details involved in the defensive scheme. Everyone, from the officers of the high command to the privates realized that a crisis was at hand…On July 5, the very day the 151st Field Artillery took its position on the line, General Naulin, commanding the 21st Army Corps, issued this order: "The attack on the Champagne front appears to be impending. I shall enter the battle with the utmost confidence…Let each one of you fight and if necessary die at his post without taking thought of what may happen upon his flanks or in the rear, and victory shall be ours."

The days of waiting immediately following were a severe strain on the men's nerves. An attack had been expected on July 6, but the fact that it did not materialize did not mean rest. As soon as the guns were in place and the caissons had been sent back to stations in the rear, the work of improving the battery positions was begun. Camouflage experts from the engineers who had been assigned to the regiments in Lorraine devised means of concealment for each battery position and took advantage of the fact that few hostile airplanes were abroad to rush the work to completion.

Appendix II

The German Attack

Shortly after midnight on July 15, the German artillery opened fire in an effort to demolish the gun positions of the Allies and thus protect their own infantry when the time came for them to go over the top…For more than three hours, the flare of a terrific artillery duel illuminated the Champagne front, during which the men of the light artillery units waited in their dugouts for the command to open fire.

These were trying hours. Camp 35, across the road from Battery E, was one of the first targets of the German artillery. Some of the horses belonging to Battery E were stabled in this camp, and the limbers and caissons of the battery were parked there. Shortly after midnight shrapnel began bursting overhead, killing some of the horses. Gas shells and more shrapnel followed. Corporal Gay E. York of Battery E received his death wound…Captain Lewis C. Coleman was severely wounded and evacuated to the hospital. Other men fell. Fifty-eight horses were killed in about twenty minutes.

A 3:45 a.m., exactly as scheduled, the German infantry crawled from its front-line trenches and began the assault. The brave French outposts who had survived the preliminary bombardment set up rocket signals, white flares with parachutes attached, which announced to men back at the guns: "The enemy is leaving his lines and advancing." Within less than a minute, a barrage from the seventy-fives and a hail of high explosives and shrapnel descended on the French first-line positions.

And now came the great moment for the 151st Field Artillery. As the Germans surged through the line of redoubts, the rocket guards caught sight of the signal, a flag rocket, which told them that the enemy was in the front of the hinterland and that the time had come for the 151st to lay down a barrage to box in those portions of the German line of attack that had penetrated the hinterland position.

The diary of Colonel Leach furnishes a graphic description of the four days of fighting on the Champaign front.

Monday, July 15: At 12 a terrific bombardment commenced and extended along a front of 100 kilometers. At 3:45 AM the Boche left their trenches and started over and 6:15 while I am writing this, they have reached the intermediate line and all our guns are going top speed. At 8:40 we started a counter attack and regaining some lost ground. Noon and we have had four guns destroyed and a good many killed and wounded and it has been a perfect hell.

Tuesday, July 16: At 12 AM while I am writing this, we have stopped the attack on our intermediary positon—we have had four killed and thirty two wounded, but have been lucky. The esprit of the Regiment has been wonderful from the start.

Wednesday, July 17: The fight let up a bit at times today and the information from the prisoners indicates that the Boche is to bring up more regiments. We have had to date forty five killed and wounded and sixty five horses killed. It is cloudy and rainy this PM and the wind is from the north and we received some gas and smoke shells.

Thursday, July 18: We are serving in the 4th French Army, 21st Corps, 13th Division. It looks today as if we have the Boche licked. Orders came tonight to fill our caissons and hold them ready which means we will leave here tomorrow, probably for another fight. At 11 PM, I received orders to leave the sector.

Aftermath of the Battle

Through the night of July 27, the regiment marched northward, wallowing in a sea of mud, drenched by rain, delayed by heavy traffic that choked the roads and exposed to shell fire and bombs…Toward the morning of July 28, the batteries of the 151st took position in the north edge of the Foret de Fere, a thick wood extending north from the wrecked town of the Beuvardes, which the Germans had abandoned that morning.

No ready-made shelters awaited the men. Gun pits were hastily dug and the men slept in holes or, in some cases, on bare ground, sheltered only by tarpaulins. The region had been held by the Germans since May. Hundreds of them still remained, but not to wage war in the cause of the All Highest. Along the roads, in open fields and in the woods they lay, some covered by shallow mounds of earth marked with wooden crosses, but many of them left unburied in the haste of their comrades' retreat before the American advance.

There were other mounds, too many of them, on which rested American rifles and American helmets; for the fight for Epieds, a quaint little French city surrounded by hills, had cost the lives of many American soldiers.

All of the towns along the way had been pommeled by shell fire when the Germans advanced in May and again during their retreat. All showed the inevitable signs of enemy occupancy—wreckage and filth. Curtains were turned down, furniture and dishes broken, closets and trunks ransacked. Bottles that had contained wine were scattered broadcast, particularly in houses that had been occupied officers.

A Very Miserable Night

The following passages from Colonel Leach's diary present a vivid picture of conditions on the front lines during the early days of August:

Monday, August 5: Went out this AM to look for a front line O.P. and had very thrilling time. The Boche saw our party and opened up with shrapnel. Returned to Chateau Thierry at 2 PM very tired. It is cold and raining, and with a bad cold and cooties I am very miserable tonight.

Tuesday, August 6: The Artillery began the preparations for the attack to cross the Vesle at noon and kept it up until 4:30 when we started a rolling barrage behind which the Infantry crossed the river and gained their objective. At midnight, we stopped a strong counter attack.

Wednesday, August 7: Holding our front all morning waiting for the right and left sectors to come up. At night we are in the same place as our flanks could not advance. Fired all night, harassing with several barrages. Am getting so tired that I can't sleep when I get a chance.

Thursday, August 8: Our right and left have not been able to advance and our Infantry have had to return several hundred meters, so the situation remains the same. The flies are getting steadily worse; and it is almost impossible to eat; even at night. Our horses are about exhausted.

Friday, August 9: The Boche are making a strong resistance north of Vesle and we have not progressed today. The brigades on the right and the left attacked but were repulsed with heavy losses. There is much dysentery on account of the flies which are getting steadily worse.

Saturday, August 10: No change in the situation today except increased enemy fire. At 4:30, we got thirty gas shells which put us to a great discomfort for a couple of hours.

Appendix II

The Roar of Battle

On September 12, zero hour came at 5:00 a.m. In all the battery positions along the St. Mihiel front, the artillery men waited anxiously for the word that should send them to the guns for the work preceding the frontal attack. The men knew the attack would come that morning. They had watched the infantry mass in second, third and fourth lines, and they had seen the tanks prepare to move forward. Ammunition had been brought to the gun positions, nightly through rain and mud.

At one o'clock [that morning] the dark and quiet St. Mihiel front changed in a few seconds into a flashing, roaring line of battle. With the German front position as the first object of attack, the light artillery rained steel and gas on trenches, dugouts and barbed-wire entanglements. In the trenches, the Alabama and Iowa infantrymen who had been designated as assault troops waited for the word to start across. Back of them, was the second wave of infantry, which had been designated to follow the third and fourth lines.

For four hours, without cessation, the tremendous concentration of fire on the German position continued, and then at five o'clock, just as day was breaking, the American infantrymen in the front line climbed out of their trenches and started forward. With them went the tanks, lumbering along through the fog of early morning, crashing through barbed wire, straddling trenches, lurching and twisting but always waddling ahead, sweeping nests with machine-gun and small shell fire.

The Germans, apparently taken by surprise, had not attempted any systematic counteroffensive firing before the attack. Apparently amazed at the thoroughness of the attack, the Germans were falling back, fighting spasmodically as they went but making no determined or effective resistance to the Americans.

As it became lighter, the fog under which the infantry [fought] disappeared, and the sun came out on the scene of battle. Observers were able to report over the wires the positions of the German soldiers who were retreating north of Essey. The heavy shelling continued until ten thirty [that morning], when information was received that the enemy was in full retreat toward the Hindenburg line.

SILENT GUNS

Under a shining sun and with regimental colors flying, the Headquarters Company of the 151st marched into Harricourt on the morning of November 10. It was the first occasion in months on which the colors had been carried at the head of the regiment.

The regiment bore grim evidence of the fighting through which it had just passed. Only twelve that remained were in pitiful condition. Many of the men were sick, and the rest were "dead on their feet."

The 151st Field Artillery was indeed "going in" again, but this time, it was to be the peaceful entrance into the land of the defeated foe.

At eleven o'clock on the morning of November 11, the firing at the front ceased and word spread that an armistice had been declared. The men and some of the officers were at first skeptical, since there had been many rumors of that sort before. There was no cheering nor excitement, though finally the conviction spread that the fighting had actually ceased. As darkness settled down, the men fired some abandoned German rocket dumps and managed to display a little enthusiasm. For the most part, however, the men were too tired for a real celebration. The fighting was ended, but the strain of the last few months had done its work. To those who had been toiling for weeks, the end of the war meant little for the time being, but warmth and sleep meant much.

NOTES

Introduction

1. The rathskeller was closed to the public in 2015 and 2016 while the capitol was undergoing renovation. The café was scheduled to reopen in 2017 at the start of that year's legislative session.
2. Holbrook and Appel, *Minnesota in the War*, 2. Holbook and Appel's two-volume history, published ten years after the end of World War I, remains the authoritative account of the war and its impact on Minnesota.

Prologue

3. *Minneapolis Tribune*, August 2, 1914, 12.
4. *St. Paul Pioneer Press*, August 1, 1914, 2.
5. Ibid.
6. Ibid., August 14, 1914, 1.
7. *Minneapolis Journal*, August 9, 1914, 4.
8. Ibid., 9.
9. *St. Peter Herald*, August 7, 1914, 10.
10. Ibid.
11. Ibid., August 14, 1914, 1.

CHAPTER 1

12. *Minneapolis Tribune*, September 13, 1914, 1.

13. Ibid.

14. Ibid., September 4, 1914, 6L.

15. *New Ulm Review*, October 14, 1914, 1.

16. *New York Times*, September 1, 1914, 2.

17. *Minneapolis Tribune*, November 8,1914, 6.

18. For an account of Wilson's Philadelphia speech, see Berg, *Wilson*, 364.

19. *Minneapolis Tribune*, May 12, 1915, 1.

20. *Minneapolis Journal*, May 8, 1914, 8.

21. *Minneapolis Tribune*, May 8, 1915, 1.

22. Ibid.

23. Ibid., 4.

24. *Minneapolis Journal*, October 10, 1916, 3.

25. Ibid., November 6, 1916, 11.

26. Ibid., October 31, 1916, 12.

27. Holbrook and Appel, *Minnesota in the War*, 47.

28. For an account of the Macalester College controversy, see Skidmore, "On Courage and Cowards."

29. Ibid.

30. *Minneapolis Tribune*, April 3, 1917, 1.

31. Ibid., April 6, 1917.

32. Ibid., April 7, 1917, 21. While Lundeen, then a Republican, was defeated in his bid for reelection in 1918, he resurfaced as a Farmer Laborite in the 1930s, was elected to the U.S. Senate in 1936 and was thought to harbor pro-Nazi sentiments at the start of World War II.

33. Ibid., April 20, 1917, 1.

34. *Minneapolis Labor Review*, April 6, 1917, 4.

CHAPTER 2

35. *Minneapolis Tribune*, April 8, 1917, D1.

36. Kennedy, *Over Here*, 147.

37. *Minneapolis Tribune*, June 3, 1917, 1.

38. Ibid., June 5, 1917, 1.

39. Holbrook and Appel, *Minnesota in the War*, 126.

40. *Minneapolis Tribune*, May 27, 1917, A4.

41. Holbrook and Appel, *Minnesota in the War*, 263.

42. Ibid., 1:189.
43. Ibid., 2:199.
44. Kennedy, *Over Here*, 105.
45. Holbrook and Appel, 223.
46. For a more complete account of shipbuilding in Duluth, see Daley, "Duluth's Other Company Town."
47. The 1916 IWW strike is described in an article by Eleff, "Minnesota Miners Strike."

CHAPTER 3

48. St. Paul's large German American community escaped the harsh measures inflicted on New Ulm by the Minnesota Public Safety Commission, but St. Paul German Americans did face serious difficulties during the war years. See Wolkerstorfer, "Persecution in St. Paul."
49. Minnesota Legislature Session Laws, 1917, chap. 261, 373–77.
50. Chrislock, *Watch Dog of Loyalty*, 60.
51. *St. Paul Daily News*, January 7, 1917, 4.
52. Chrislock, *Watchdog of Loyalty*, 77, 78.
53. Ibid.
54. Millikan, "Minneapolis Civic and Commerce Association."
55. *New Ulm Review*, August 1, 1917, 1.
56. Ibid.
57. *Princeton Union*, July 26, 1917, 4.
58. Ibid., August 16, 1917, 4.
59. Chrislock, *Watchdog of Loyalty*, 139.
60. *New Ulm Review*, August 29, 1917, 1.
61. Ibid., August 22, 1917, 4.
62. Ibid.
63. Ibid.
64. *St. Paul Pioneer Press*, October 7, 1917, 1.
65. *Minneapolis Labor Review*, October 12, 1917, 1.
66. *St. Paul Pioneer Press*, December 3, 1917, 1.
67. Chrislock, *Watchdog of Loyalty*, 184–86.
68. St. Paul Trades and Labor Assembly, "Truth About the Street Car Troubles."

Chapter 4

69. *Minneapolis Journal*, April 5, 1918, 1.
70. Ibid., April 11, 1918, 1.
71. *St. Paul Pioneer Press*, April 1, 1918, 1.
72. *Duluth News Tribune*, April 2, 1918, 11.
73. *Mankato Free Press*, April 5, 1918, 1.
74. Ibid.
75. *St. Paul Pioneer Press*, April 3, 1918, 1.
76. *Minneapolis Journal*, April 7, 1918, 1.
77. *St. Paul Pioneer Press*, April 6, 1918, 6.
78. Ibid., April 7, 1918, 4.
79. *Minneapolis Journal*, April 5, 1918, 17.
80. Ibid.
81. Ibid., April 4, 1918, 9.
82. *St. Paul Pioneer Press*, April 8, 1918.
83. *Minneapolis Journal*, April 1, 1918, 1.
84. Holbrook, *St. Paul and Ramsey County*, 95–96.

Chapter 5

85. *Minneapolis Journal*, April 4, 1918, 17.
86. Lindbergh, *Why Your Country Is at War*, 7.
87. Chrislock, *Progressive Era in Minnesota*, 167.
88. Ibid., 165.
89. *Minneapolis Tribune*, March 12, 1918, 1.
90. Chrislock, *Progressive Era in Minnesota*, 169–70.
91. Ibid.
92. Jenson, "Loyalty as a Political Weapon," 55.
93. The NPL's legacy is still recognized in North Dakota, where that state's Democratic Party organization has incorporated the NPL in its name and calls itself the Democratic Nonpartisan League Party.
94. *Minneapolis Labor Review*, October 30, 1914, 1. For a more extensive account of Thomas Van Lear's political career, see Nathanson, "Thomas Van Lear."
95. Nord, "Minneapolis and the Pragmatic Socialism of Thomas Van Lear," 4.
96. *Minneapolis Tribune*, November 6, 1916, 4.
97. Kennedy, *Over Here*, 26.
98. *Minneapolis Labor Review*.

99. *Minneapolis Tribune*, November 1, 1917, 15.

100. Ibid., August 10, 1917, 1.

101. *Minneapolis Labor Review*, October 5, 1917, 1.

102. *Minneapolis Tribune*, October 11, 1917, 10.

103. Ibid., April 18, 1917, 14.

104. *Minneapolis Labor Review*, May 24, 1918, 2.

105. *Minneapolis Tribune*, May 16, 1918, 1.

106. Ibid., May 20, 1917, 1.

107. Ibid., November 8, 1918, 16. Van Lear made one more effort at a comeback in 1921 but narrowly lost the mayoralty race to George Leach, a war hero who commanded Minnesota's 151st Field Artillery.

Chapter 6

108. Dowd, "Spanish Influenza in St. Paul," 19–23.

109. Ibid., 19.

110. Haddy, *Country Doctor and City Doctor*, 134–35.

111. *Minneapolis Tribune*, October 1, 1918, 14.

112. Ibid., October 4, 1918, 1.

113. *Minneapolis Journal*, October 11, 1918, 2.

114. Haddy, *Country Doctor and City Doctor*, 132.

115. Filzen, "Influenza Pandemic of 1918."

116. *Minneapolis Journal*, October 12, 1918, 1.

117. *St. Paul Pioneer Press*, November 3, 1918, 4.

118. Ibid., November 4, 1918, 1.

119. *Journal of the American Medical Association* 71, no. 11, 809.

120. *Minneapolis Journal*, October 12, 1918, 1.

121. *New Prague Times*, November 7, 1918, 1.

122. *Daily Post and Record*, November 11, 1918, 1.

123. *Winona Republican Herald*, November 12, 1918, 5.

124. *Minneapolis Journal*, November 11, 1918, 1.

125. *Minneapolis Tribune*, November 11, 1918, 1.

126. Collins, *History of the 151st Field Artillery*.

127. Leach, *War Dairies*, 203.

Epilogue

128. Wirth, *Minneapolis Park System*, 144.
129. Dedication program for Victory Memorial Drive on June 12, 1921, in the archives of the Hennepin County Special Collection.
130. Ibid.

BIBLIOGRAPHY

Berg, A. Scott. *Wilson*. New York: G.P. Putnam's Sons, 2013.

Chrislock, Carl. *The Progressive Era in Minnesota, 1915–22*. St. Paul: Minnesota Historical Society, 1971.

———. *Watch Dog of Loyalty: The Minnesota Commission of Public Safety During World War I*. St. Paul: Minnesota Historical Society Press, 1991.

Collins, Louis L. *History of the 151st Field Artillery*. St. Paul: Minnesota War Records Commission, 1924

Cooper, John Milton. *Pivotal Decades, United States, 1900–1920*. New York: W.W. Norton & Company, 1990.

Daley, Matthew Lawrence. "Duluth's Other Company Town." *Minnesota History*, Spring 2013.

Dowd, Susan. "The Spanish Influenza in St. Paul in 1918, the Year the City Found the Wolf at Its Door." *Ramsey County History* 40, no. 1 (Spring 2004).

Eighmey, Ray Katherine. *Food Will Win the War*. St. Paul: Minnesota Historical Society Press, 2010.

Eleff, Robert M. "The Minnesota Miners Strike Against U.S. Steel." *Minnesota History*, Summer 1988.

Filzen, Darlene. "The Influenza Pandemic of 1918: An Overview and Its Effect on Brown County." Unpublished manuscript in the Minnesota Historical Society archives.

Haddy, Theresa Brey. *Country Doctor and City Doctor*. Edina, MN: Beavers Pond Press, 2006.

Hoisington, Daniel J. *A History of New Ulm*. New Ulm, MN: City of New Ulm, 2004.

Holbrook, Franklin F. *St. Paul and Ramsey County in the War of 1917–18*. St. Paul: Ramsey County War Records Commission, 1929.

Holbrook, Franklin, and Livia Appel. *Minnesota in the War with Germany*. Vol. 1. St. Paul: Minnesota Historical Society, 1928.

Jenson, Carol. "Loyalty as a Political Weapon: The 1918 Campaign in Minnesota." *Minnesota History*, Summer 1971.

Journal of the American Medical Association 71, no. 11.

Kennedy David M. *Over Here: The First World War and American Society*. New York: Oxford University Press, 2004.

Larson, Bruce L. *Lindbergh of Minnesota: A Political Biography*. New York: Harcourt Brace Jovanovich, 1973.

Leach, George. *War Diaries*. N.p., 1923.

Lee, Art. "Hometown Hysteria, Bemidji at the Start of World War I." *Minnesota History*, Summer 1984.

Lindbergh, Charles. *Why Your Country Is at War*. Washington, D.C., 1917.

Millikan, William. "The Minneapolis Civic and Commerce Association Versus Labor During World War I." *Minnesota History*, Spring 1986.

Minnesota Legislature Session Laws, 1917.

Nathanson, Iric. "Thomas Van Lear, City Hall's Working-Class Champion." *Minnesota History*, Summer 1915.

Nord, David Paul. "Minneapolis and the Pragmatic Socialism of Thomas Van Lear." *Minnesota History*, Spring 1976.

Skidmore, Emily. "On Courage and Cowards, the Controversy Surrounding the Macalester College Neutrality and Peace Association, 1917." *Ramsey County History* 43, no. 2.

St. Paul Trades and Labor Assembly. "The Truth About the Street Car Troubles." St. Paul, MN, 1919.

Wirth, Theodore. *The Minneapolis Park System 1883–1944*. Minneapolis, MN: Minneapolis Board of Park Commissioners, 1944.

Wolkerstorfer, Sister John Christine. "Persecution in St Paul: The Germans in World War I." *Ramsey County History* 13, no. 1 (Fall 1976).

INDEX

ABOUT THE AUTHOR

Iric Nathanson writes and lectures about Minnesota history. His articles have appeared in a variety of publications including *Minnesota History*, *Hennepin History*, the *Star Tribune* and the online daily *MinnPost*. His 2010 book, *Minneapolis in the Twentieth Century*, was a finalist for the Minnesota Book Award. *The Minneapolis Riverfront*, his 2014 book, was published by Arcadia Publishing as part of its Images of America Series.